Caught *in the* Act

Garry Winogrand. *Apollo 11
Moon Shot, Cape Kennedy,
Florida, 1969.* Gelatin silver

Caught *in the* Act

THE PHOTOGRAPHER IN CONTEMPORARY FICTION

EDITED BY BARRY MUNGER

t Timken Publishers

Timken Publishers, Inc.
137 Varick Street
New York, NY 10013

LIBRARY OF CONGRESS CATALOGUING-IN-PUBLICATION DATA
Caught in the act : the photographer in contemporary fiction / edited
   by Barry Munger
        p.   cm.
    ISBN 0-943221-27-7
    1. Photographers—Fiction. 2. Short stories. I. Munger, Barry,
    1900–
    IN PROCESS
    808.83'99277—dc20   96–23291
                                                      CIP

Typeset in Adobe Caslon and Gill Sans
Cover and text designed and produced by David Bullen
Copyedited by Anna Jardine
Printed in the United States of America

Contents

Walker Evans. *Resort Photographer at Work, Florida,* 1941. **Gelatin silver print.** (The Metropolitan Museum of Art, Gift of Arnold H. Crane, 1972 (1972.742.25). Copyright © Walker Evans Archive, The Metropolitan Museum of Art)

The Guilty Bystander

Every picture tells a story, but there is also a story behind every picture, as anyone who has spent time in the company of photographers can tell you.

Newcomers to the medium quickly learn that photographers' stories are a lot like fishermen's: they tend to celebrate lucky snags and persistence; strange intuitions about their quarry and the weather; and inevitably, the one that got away.

Such material can be the stuff of great literature. The fisherman's story, after all, has a tradition stretching from *Moby-Dick* to Norman Maclean's "A River Runs Through It." As this collection shows, the photographer's quest is just as ripe with narrative possibility, and has inspired fictions both comic and tragic, slice-of-life and fantastic, straightforward and elliptical.

However varied in approach, the stories gathered here share one trait: a suspicion that the photographer, unlike the average fisherman, is morally adrift. This unmoored quality is often disguised – it appears as arrogance in "The Image Trade," as aloofness in "Greene" and "Lies," and as a mania for image gathering in "Highspeed Linear Main St." and "The Adventures of the Photographer" – but it can also manifest itself in overtly criminal behavior, as in "Billy Ducks Among the Pharaohs" and "Negatives."

Even in stories in which photographers show great moral sensitivity, such as "Shots" and "Blow-Up," their devotion to the medium is a symptom of metaphysical unease. Like the detached narrator of Camus's *The Fall*, who strolls past a suicide, the photographers in these stories watch unfolding crimes through their camera viewfinders. How such proximity implicates them is far from clear, but there is no doubt about the taint; with each snap of the shutter, the photographers capture a moment of ineffable evil, slice the apple of original sin.

The note of ambivalence in this collection is not an editorial imposition. The selection process sought diversity, including a wide range of photographers, from a novice traveling door to door, to a hard-bitten paparazzo; from a celebrity portraitist, to documenters of roadside kitsch and rural poverty.

Still, a certain darkness remained, and from that darkness came the shadowy back-street figure on the cover, as well as the title, with its overtone of surprised transgression. The photographers chronicled here are also "caught in the act" in a more benign sense: they are shown at work, entangled in theater, immersed in their craft.

Photographers become photographers for any number of reasons. Many are drawn by the medium's mechanical and chemical wonders, since both the taking and the printing of photographs have a pleasing precision. Those immune to the physical beauty of cameras, or the marvel of an image forming on a sheet of blank paper, are not likely to become photographers.

Others want to knock around, meet the meek and powerful, seize a bit of the world's hurly-burly. After all, traveling around taking pictures is what most people do on their vacations, and many photographers retain a sense of privilege for being paid for their pleasure.

Whatever brings them to the vocation, photographers are eventually influenced by the work of others, and most photographers remember the first work that impressed them with the medium's potential. For Garry Winogrand (see frontispiece), it was the work of

Walker Evans (see page vi). Although he had been a professional photographer for years, Winogrand was awed when he first saw Evans's book *American Photographs*. "That is the first time I was ever moved by photographs," he said. "I don't mean that I wanted to cry; I don't mean that by 'being moved.' It's the first time I was aware that photographs themselves could describe intelligence."

As it happens, the first photographs that had that effect on me were Garry Winogrand's. I was a sophomore in college, and I was attracted by his photographs' animal physicality, insouciance, and satiric edge. His pictures made me laugh.

And yet they were clearly the work of an urban predator, a man wandering the streets imposing himself on strangers, snaring them in moments of absurdity. As trespasses go, his were minor: the subjects were often caught unaware, and in any case, their discomfort seldom lasted longer than 1/125 of a second. Still, when I first tried "street photography," as the practice is called, I was often struck by the similarity between my activities, ostensibly so noble and sophisticated, and those of the virulent tourist, the creep, and the voyeur.

Every photographer faces qualms of this sort, and changing working methods only changes the qualms. One is not always sure whether one is exploring or exploiting, documenting or manipulating, embracing or intruding. It may be true, as Ezra Pound wrote, that "fundamental accuracy of statement is the ONE sole morality of writing," but in photography, accuracy is often assumed, and moral scrutiny tends to focus on the photographer's motives.

By Pound's standard, the stories in this collection are moral, in that each of them has something fundamentally accurate to say about photographers and photography. Furthermore, the stories engage ethical issues that often lurk unacknowledged in the commerce of "the image trade," as V. S. Pritchett calls it.

The morality of photographs, on the other hand, is a slippery issue, and one photograph in particular always makes me conscious of that fact. It's in Robert Frank's *The Americans*. Like many photographers, I know this book well and regard it as a family album of my country, but I have no special knowledge of the photograph in question.

It is called "Car Accident – U.S. 66, Between Winslow and Flagstaff, Arizona," and it shows four people standing on a weedy rise beside a highway, contemplating what appears to be a corpse or corpses shrouded in a blanket. There are no crushed cars visible. The image has a stark, existential formality that makes it seem less like a photograph of an accident than a symbol of one, a totem of "the mad road, lonely, leading around the bend into the openings of space towards the horizon," as Jack Kerouac wrote in the book's introduction.

Imagine yourself at this scene in 1955, however. The shrouded form is not a symbol. It is a corpse, and you are standing beside it on Route 66 in Arizona and it is cold. Perhaps you have come from your house. A car pulls by, slowly, and stops. A stranger gets out, and you hear his feet in the gravel. He stands on the shoulder staring at you, and then raises a camera, framing you, and you feel yourself pass into geometry. How could you possibly recognize the stranger for what he is – an emissary of sentiment and history?

Barry Munger

Caught *in the* Act

Allen Ginsberg. *Robert Frank's*
Bleecker Street Studio, New York
City, **1984. Gelatin silver print.**
Photograph by Allen Ginsberg as
taken by Peter Orlovsky.
(Courtesy Fahey/Klein Gallery, Los
Angeles. Copyright © 1994 Allen
Ginsberg)

The Image Trade

V. S. PRITCHETT

What do you make of the famous Zut – I mean his stuff in this exhibition? Is he just a newsy collector of human instances jellied in his darkroom, or is he an artist – a Zurbarán, say, a priest searching another priest's soul? Pearson, one of a crowd of persons, was silently putting these questions to them on a London bus going north.

Last July, Pearson went on, he was at home. The front-door bell rang. "He's here! On time!" his beautiful wife said. She was scraping the remains of his hair across his scalp. "Wait," she said, and turning him round, she gave a last sharp brush to his shoulders and sent him dibble-dabbing fast down three flights of stairs to the door. There stood Zut, the photographer, with his back to Pearson and on impatient feet, tall and thin in a suit creased by years of air travel. He was shouting to Mrs. Zut, who was lugging two heavy bags of apparatus up the street to the house. She got there and they turned round.

As a writer, in the news too and in another branch of the human-image trade, Pearson depended on seeing people and things as strictly they are not. The notion that Zut and his wife could be a doorstep couple offering to buy old spectacles or discarded false teeth, a London trade, occurred to him, but he recovered and, switching on an eager smile, bowed them into the house. They marched past him down the hall, briskly, like a pair of surgeons, to the foot of the stairs and looked back at him.

"I hope you had no difficulty in finding this – er – place," Pearson said, vain of difficulty as a sort of fame.

3

"None," said Zut. "She drives. I read the street map." Mrs. Zut had not put down her load. Zut seemed to ask, Are you the body?

Well, said Pearson spaciously, where did they want to "do," or "take" – he hesitated between saying "it" or "me." He said this to all photographers, waving a hand, offering the house. Zut looked up at the stairs and the high ceiling.

Pearson said, Ground-floor dining room, tall windows, books? Upstairs by half-landing, a balcony, or would you say patio, flowers, shrubs, greenery, a pair of Chinese dogs in stone, view of neighboring gardens? Down below, garden seat under tree, could sit there taking the air. And talking of air, have often been done – if that is the word – outside in the street, in overcoat and fur hat by interesting railings, coat buttoned or unbuttoned. No? Or first-floor sitting room. High windows again, fourteen feet in fact, expensive when curtaining, but chairs easy or uneasy, large mirror, peacock feathers on wife's desk, quite a lot of gilt, *chaise-longue* indeed. Have often been done there, upright or lying full length. *Death of Chatterton* style.

Zut said, "Furniture tells me nothing. Where do you work?"

"Work?" said Pearson.

"Where you write," said Zut.

"Oh, that," said Pearson. "You mean the alphabet, sentences? At the top. Three flights up, I'm afraid," apologizing to Mrs. Zut. (Writer, writing at desk, rather a cliché for a man like Zut – no?)

Already Zut was taking long steps up the stairs, followed by Mrs. Zut, who refused to give up her two rattling bags, Pearson looking at Mrs. Zut's gray hair and peaceful back as he came after them. From flight to flight they went and did not speak until they were under a fanlight at the top. In a pause for breath Pearson said, "Burglar's entry."

Zut ignored this and, pointing to a door, "In here?" he said.

"No, used to be children's bathroom. Other door." The door was white on the outside, yellowing on the inside. They marched in.

"It smells of – what would you say? – decaying rhubarb, I'm afraid. I smoke a pipe."

There was the glitter of permafrost in Zut's hunting eyes as he studied the room. There were two attic windows; the other three walls were blood-red but stacked and stuffed with books to the ceiling. They were terraced like a football crowd, in varieties of anoraks, a crowd unstirred by a slow game going on among four tables where more books and manuscripts were in scrimmage.

"That your desk?" said Zut, pointing to the largest table.

"I'm a table man," said Pearson, apologizing, bending to pick up one or two matches and a paper clip from the floor. "I migrate from table to table." And drew attention to a large capsized photograph of the Albert Memorial propped on a chest of drawers. Accidentally, Zut kicked a metal wastepaper basket as he looked round. It gave a knell.

Yes, Pearson was inclined to say (but did not), this room has a knell. Authors die. Dozens of funerals of unfinished sentences here every day. It is less a study than a – what shall I say? – perhaps a dockyard for damaged syntax? Or, better still, an immigration hall. Papers arrive at a table, migrate to other tables or chairs, and, when they are rubber-stamped, get stuffed into drawers. By the way, outgoing mail on the floor. Observe the corner bookcase, the final catacomb – my file boxes. I like to forget.

Mrs. Zut dropped to her knees near a window and was opening the bags.

Now (Pearson was offering his body to Zut), what would you like me to be or do? Stand here? Or there? Sit? Left leg crossed over right leg, right over left? Put on a look? Get a book at random? Open a drawer? Light a pipe? Talk? Think? Put hand on chin? Great Zut, make your wish known.

Talk, Zut. All photographers talk, put client at ease. Ask me questions. Dozens of pictures of me have been taken. I could show you my early slim-subaltern-on-the-Somme-waiting-to-go-over-the-top period. There was my Popular Front look in the Thirties and Forties, the jersey-wearing, all-the-world's-a-coal-mine period, with close-ups of the pores and scars of the skin and the gleam of sweat. There was the editorial look, when the tailor had to let out the waist of my trousers, followed by the successful smirk. In the Sixties the plunging neckline, no tie. Then back to collar and tie in my failed-bronze-Olympic period. Today, I fascinate archaeologists – you know, the broken pillar of a lost civilization. Come on, Zut. What do you want?

Zut looked at the largest table. It had a clear space among pots of pencils, ashtrays, paper clips, two piles of folders for the execution block – a large blotter embroidered by pen wipings, and on it was a board with beautiful clean white paper clipped to it.

"There," said Zut, pointing to the chair in front of it. Zut had swollen veins on his long hands. "Sit," he said.

Pearson sat. There was a hiss from Mrs. Zut's place on the floor, close to Zut. She had pulled out the steel rods of a whistling tripod. Zut gave a push to her shoulder. Up came a camera. She screwed it on and Zut fiddled with it, calling for more and more little things. What fun you have in your branch of the trade, said Pearson. You have little things to twizzle. Well, I have paper clips, pipe cleaners, scissors, paste. I try out pens, that's all – to save me from entering the wilderness, the wilderness of vocabulary.

But now Zut was pulling his creased jacket over his head and squinting through the camera at Pearson, who felt a small flake of his face fall off. And at that moment Zut gave Mrs. Zut a knock on her arm. "Meter," he said. Then he let his coat slip back to his shoulders and stepped from the end of the table to where Pearson was sitting and held the meter, with shocking intimacy, close to Pearson's head. He looked back at the window, muttering a word. Was the word "unclean"? And he turned to squint through the camera and looked up to say, "Take your glasses off."

My glasses. My only defense. Can't see a thing. He took them off.

Ah, Zut, I see you don't talk, because you are after the naked truth, you are a dabbler in the puddles of the mind. As you like, but I warn you I'm wise to that.

"Don't smile."

I see, you're not a smile-please man, muttered Pearson. Oh, Zut, you've such a shriven look. If you take me naked, you will miss all the *et cetera* of my life. I am all *et cetera*. But Zut was back under his jacket, spying again, and then he did something presumptuous. He came out of his jacket, reached across the table, and moved a pot of pencils out of the way. The blue pot, that rather pretty *et cetera* that Pearson's wife had found in a junk shop next to the butcher's – now a pizza café – twenty-four years ago on a street not in this district. Zut, you have moved a part of my life to another table, it will hate being there, screamed Pearson's soul. How dare you move my wife?

Anything else?

"Not necessary," said Zut, and reaching out, gave Mrs. Zut a knock on the arm. "Lamp," he said between his teeth.

Mrs. Zut scrabbled in the bag and pulled out a rubbery cord; at the end was a clouded yellow lamp, a small sickly moon. She stood up and held it high.

Zut gave another knock on her arm as he spied into the camera.

"Higher," he said.

Up went the lamp. Another knock.

"Keep still. You're letting it droop," said Zut. Oh, Florence Nightingale, can't you, after all these years, hold it steady?

"Look straight into the camera," called Zut from under his jacket.

"Now write," said Zut.

"Write? Where?"

"On that paper."

"Pen or pencil?" said Pearson. "Write what?"

"Anything."

"Like at school."

Pearson tipped the board on the edge of the table.

"Don't tip the board. Keep it flat."

"I can't write flat. I never write flat," Pearson said. And I never write in public, if anyone is in the room. I grunt. I make a noise.

I bet you can't photograph a noise.

Pearson glanced at Zut. Then, sulking, he slid the board back flat on the table and felt the room tip up.

Zut, Pearson murmured. I shall write: Zut keeps on hitting his wife. Zut keeps on hitting his wife. Can't write that. He might see. Zut, I am going to diddle you. I shall write my address, 56 Hill Road Terrace, with the wrong post code – N64DN. Here goes: 56 Hill Road Terrace, 56 Hill Road Terrace . . .

"Keep on writing," said Zut.

Pearson continued 56 Hill Road Terrace and then misspelled "terrace." Out of the corner of his eye he saw the little yellow lamp.

"Now look up at me," said Zut.

The room tipped higher.

"Like that. Like that. Like that," hissed Zut. "Go on. Now go on writing."

Click, click, click, went the shutter of the camera. A little toad in the lens has shot out a long tongue and caught a fly.

"You're dropping it again," said Zut, giving Mrs. Zut a punch.

"Good," the passionate Zut called to Pearson, then came out of his jacket.

"My face has gone," Pearson said.

But how do you know you've got *me*? My soul spreads all over my body, even in my feet. My face is nothing. At my age I don't need it. It is no more than a servant I push around before me. Or a football I kick ahead of me, taking all the blows, in shops, in the streets. It knows nothing. It just collects. I send it to smirk at parties, to give lectures. It has a mouth. I've no idea what it says. It calls people by the wrong names. It is an indiscriminate little grinner. It kisses people I've never met. The only time my face and I exchange a word is when I shave. Then it sulks.

Click, went the camera.

Pearson sat back and put down his pen and dropped his arm to his side.

"Will you do that again," said Zut. "The way you just dropped your arm," Zut said.

Pearson did it.

"No," said Zut. "We've missed it."

Pearson was hurt, and apologized to Mrs. Zut, the dumb goddess. Not for worlds would he upset her husband. She simply gazed at Zut.

Zut himself straightened up. The room tipped back to its normal state. Pearson noticed the long lines down the sides of Zut's mouth, wondered why the jacket did not rumple his gray hair. Cropped, of course. How old was he? Where had he flown from? Hovering vulture. Unfortunate Satan walking up and down the world looking for souls. Satan on his treadmill. I bet your father was in, say, the clock trade, was it? – and when you were a boy you took his watch to pieces looking for Time. Why don't you *talk*? You're not like that man who came here last year and told me that he waited until he felt there was a magnetic flow uniting himself and me. A technological flirt. Nor are you like that other happy fellow with the waving fair hair who said he unselfed himself, forgot money, wife, children, all, for a few seconds to become me!

Zut slid a new plate into the camera and glanced up at the ceiling. It was smudged by the faint shadows of the beams behind it. A prison or cage effect. Why was he looking at the ceiling? Did he want it to be removed?

Pearson said, "Painted only five years ago. And look at it! More expense."

Zut dismissed this.

"Look towards the window," said Zut.

"Which one?" said Pearson.

"On the right," said Zut. "Yes. Yes." Another blow on that poor woman's arm.

"Lamp – higher. Still higher."

Click, click from the toad in the lens.

"Again," said Zut.

Click. Click. Another click.

"Ah!" said Zut, as if about to faint.

He's found something at last, Pearson thought. But Zut, I bet you don't know where my mind was. No, I was not looking at the tree-tops. I was looking at a particular branch. On a still day like this, there is always one leaf skipping about at the end of a branch on its own while the rest of the tree is still. It has been doing that for years. Why? An *et cetera*, a distinguished leaf. Could be me. What am I but a leaf?

One more halfhearted click from the camera, and then Zut stood tall. He had achieved boredom.

"I've got all I want," he muttered sharply to his wife.

All? said Pearson, appealing. There are tons of me left. I know I have a face like a cup of soup with handles sticking out – you know? – after it has been given a couple of stirs with a wooden spoon. A speciality in a way. What wouldn't I give for bone structure, a nose with bone in it!

Zut gave a last dismissive look around the room.

"That's it," he said to his wife.

She started to dismantle the tripod. Zut walked to the photograph of the Albert Memorial on the chest near the door, done by another photographer, and studied it. There was an enormous elephant's head in the foreground. Zut pointed. "Only one eye," he said censoriously.

"The other's in shadow," said Pearson.

"Elephants have two eyes," said Zut. And then, "Is there a . . ."

"Of course, of course, the door on the left."

Pearson was putting the muscles of his face back in place. He was alone with Mrs. Zut, who was packing up the debris of the hour.

"I have always admired your husband's work," he said politely.

"Thank you," she said from the floor, buckling the bags.

"Remarkable pictures of men – and, of course, women. I think I saw one of you, didn't I, in his last collection?"

"No," she said from the floor, looking proud. "I don't allow him to take my picture."

"Oh surely –"

"No," she said, the whole of herself standing up, full-faced, solid and human.

"His first wife, yes. Not me," she said resolutely, killing the other in the ordinary course of life.

Then Zut came back, and in procession they all began thanking their way downstairs to the door.

At the exhibition Pearson sneaked in to see himself, stayed ten minutes to look at his portrait, and came out screaming, thinking of Mrs. Zut.

An artist, he said. Herod! he was shouting. When the head of John the Baptist was handed to you on that platter, the eyes of that beautiful severed head were peacefully closed. But what do I see at the bottom of your picture. A high haunted room whose books topple. Not a room indeed, but a dank cistern or aquarium of stale water. No sparkling anemone there but the bald head of a melancholy frog, its feet clinging to a log, floating in literature. O Fame, cried Pearson, O Maupassant, O *Tales of Hoffmann*, O Edgar Allan Poe, O Grub Street.

Pearson rushed out and rejoined the human race on that bus going north and sat silently addressing the passengers, the women particularly, who all looked like Mrs. Zut. The sight of them changed his mind. He was used, he said, to his face gallivanting with other ladies and gentlemen, in newspapers, books, and occasionally on the walls of galleries like that one down the street. Back down the street, he said, a man called Zut, a photographer, an artist, not one of your click-click men, had exhibited his picture, but by a mysterious accident of art had portrayed his soul instead of mine. What faces, Pearson said, that poor fellow must see just before he drops off to sleep at night beside the wise woman who won't let him take a picture of her, fearing perhaps the Evil Eye. A man in the image trade, like myself, Pearson called back as he got off the bus. Not a Zurbarán, more a Hieronymus Bosch perhaps. No one noticed Pearson getting off.

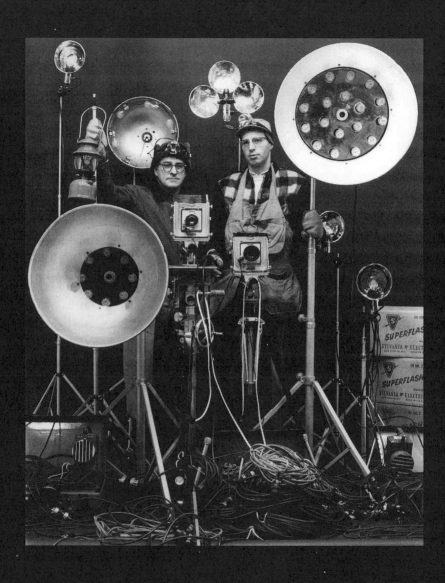

O. Winston Link. *Link and Thom and Night Flash Equipment*, 1956. **Gelatin silver print.** (Copyright © O. Winston Link)

Billy Ducks Among the Pharaohs

RICK DeMARINIS

The Billetdoux front yard should have told me right away that the job wouldn't amount to much. The lawn was overgrown with spiky weeds, what grass there was had died a number of seasons ago, deep tire ruts oozy with muck grooved the yard, and a rusty tub filled with crankcase oil sat on the warped porch. But I had just turned eighteen and was still untuned to the distress signals the world volunteers with unfailing reliability.

Price Billetdoux – he pronounced his name "Billy Ducks" – answered my knock. He was in pajamas and bathrobe, even though it was midafternoon. He stood before me, dark and grizzled, blinded by ordinary daylight. When he focused on me, he shoved his hand into his robe pocket as if looking for a gun.

"I'm the one who called," I explained quickly. I held up the newspaper and pointed to his ad. "I want to try it, photography."

"Amigo," he said, pulling a crumpled pack of Camels from his bathrobe, "come in."

I followed him into the kitchen. There was a plump girl at the stove peeling an egg off a skillet. She was also in pajamas and robe. She had stringy, mud-colored hair and very small feet. She looked about twelve. I figured she was Billetdoux's daughter.

15

"Pour us a couple of cups of java, will you, Shyanne?" he said to her.

The girl dragged two cups out of the sink, rinsed them, and filled them with inky coffee. She moved listlessly, as if she had been sick and was just recovering.

Billetdoux lit his Camel, drank some coffee, made a face. He had haggard, bloodshot eyes. Dark, tender-looking pouches hung like pulpy half-moons under them. He squinted at me through the smoke, sizing me up. Then he explained the job. No salary. No insurance. No fringe benefits. No vacations. Everything I made would be a percentage of the gross. I would go from door to door, trying to get housewives to let me take pictures of them and their children. I would offer them an eight-by-ten glossy for only one dollar. That was the "bait." How could they refuse? But when I went back with the print, I would also have a portfolio of five-by-sevens, three-by-fives, plus a packet of wallet-size prints. The portfolio would cost anywhere from $5.95 to $11.95, depending on how many prints were purchased. Of course, if they accepted only the eight-by-ten "bait" item for a buck, there was no profit or commission.

"You can make a hundred or more a week if you're good," Billetdoux said. "And your hours are your own. I've got a boy over in Sulphur Springs who nets one-fifty."

I admitted that I didn't know the first thing about taking pictures, but he fanned the air between us as if to not only clear the cigarette smoke but also the heavy cobwebs of confusion from my mind. "I can show you how to take pictures of a prize-winning quality in ten minutes, amigo. The job, however, is salesmanship, not art."

He took me down to the basement where he kept his "photolab." We had to pass through a hall that led to the back of the house. Halfway down the hall he stopped next to a door and tapped on it softly. Then he pushed it open an inch. I saw a woman with wild gray hair lying in bed. She was propped up on several pillows. She also had the sickroom look, just as the girl did. Her eyes were dark and lusterless and her skin looked like damp paper. There was a guitar lying across her lap.

"I've got to break in a new boy, Lona," Billetdoux said. "I'll get you some breakfast in a little bit." Lona, who I assumed was Billetdoux's wife, let her head loll off the pillows until she was facing us. She didn't speak, but her large, drugged-looking eyes seemed to be nursing specific, long-term resentments. After Billetdoux closed the door, he whispered, "Lona is very creative, amigo."

The basement was a hodge-podge of equipment, stacked boxes, file cabinets, work tables, half-finished carpentry projects, all of it permeated with the smell of chemicals. He shoved stacks of paper around on his desk until he found a small brass key. He opened a cabinet with this key and took out a camera. "We'll start you on the Argus," he said. "It's simple to use and takes a decent picture. Later on, if you stick with me, I'll check you out on a Rolleiflex."

He took me step by step through the Argus, from film loading to f-stop and shutter speed. "I'll go around with you the first few days," he said, "to show you the ropes. Then you're on your own. You're a nice-looking boy – the housewives will trust you." He winked, as if to suggest that trusting the likes of me and Billetdoux would be the biggest blunder a housewife could make.

We went back upstairs to the kitchen. "How about some breakfast?" he said.

I looked at my watch. "It's after three," I said.

"It is? No wonder I'm so hungry. Where the hell does the time run off to, amigo? Well, how about some lunch then? Could you go for a bite of lunch?"

"Sure," I said. I hadn't eaten breakfast either.

"Shyanne," he called. "Honey, would you come in here?"

She came in, looking slightly more haggard than when I first saw her.

"Shy, hon, fix us some lunch, will you? The boy here and I are starved."

"There's no bread," she said. "Or meat."

Billetdoux pulled open a cupboard door. "How about some Cheerios, then?" he said.

"Fine by me," I said.

He poured out three bowls of the cereal, then added milk. He handed one bowl to Shyanne. "Here, hon," he said. "Take this in to Lona, will you? She hasn't eaten since yesterday."

"No one's eaten since yesterday," she said. "Except me, if you want to count that measly egg."

Billetdoux grinned darkly at me, embarrassed. "Time to make a grocery run, I guess," he said.

We ate in silence. The milk on my cereal was slightly sour. A big late-summer fly droned past my ear and landed upside down on the table where it exercised its thick, feeble legs. A loud, nasty voice broke into the homely sound of our spoons tapping on the Melmac bowls. I heard the word "swill" hiss from the hallway. Shyanne came in, carrying the bowl of Cheerios. "Lona doesn't want cereal," she said, dumping the milk-bloated O's into the sink. "She wants Spam and eggs."

"What about toast?" Billetdoux said.

"Right. Toast, too, and hashbrowns."

He leaned forward, his eyes damp and tired-looking. "Listen, kid," he said. "Can you loan me ten bucks until tomorrow? I'm a little short. I had to get a new transmission put in my car last week. Cost? It's legal robbery."

I took out my wallet. I still had about fifty dollars from my last job. I gave him ten.

"Thanks, amigo. Splendid. I won't forget this. This is above and beyond, amigo."

Shyanne plucked the ten out of his hand. "I'll go to the store," she said.

"Don't forget cigarettes," Billetdoux said.

Billetdoux told me how to snowjob a housewife, but the first door we knocked at was answered by a kid of about six or seven. I looked at Billetdoux, who was standing right behind me. "What do I do now?" I asked.

"Is your old lady at home, buster?" Billetdoux said.

The kid started to close the door. His little sister, naked and grimy, stood behind him, a gray pork chop in her muddy hand. Pale green bulbs of snot plugged her nostrils.

Billetdoux pulled a bent Tootsie Roll out of his pocket and gave it to the boy. The boy accepted it, visibly relaxing his doorway vigil. "Mummy not home, huh?" Billetdoux said. "Well, that's all right. That's no problem at all." To me he whispered, "In a way, amigo, it makes our job easier."

He pushed the door all the way open and we went in. "Set the flood lamps up like I told you," he said. "Remember, the mainlight sits back about seven feet. Put the fill-light about three feet behind it, but over to the right. That way we get an arty shadow."

I opened the equipment case I'd carried in and took out the lamps. I set them up on their stands. While I was doing this, Billetdoux set two chairs up in the middle of the living room. I moved the two lamps so that they were the proper distance from the chairs.

"Hey, buster," Billetdoux said to the boy. "Your sis got any clothes? Why don't you be a good scout and hunt up some drawers for her, okay? We don't want to take what you might call filthy pornographic pictures, do we? And wash off her snot-locker while you're at it."

I set up the tripod and attached the Argus to it. The boy pulled a pair of pink panties on his sister. I took the pork chop out of her hand

and set it on the coffee table. I used my own handkerchief to clean her nose. Billetdoux sat them down in the chairs. He stepped back and looked at them in the unmerciful blare of the flood lamps. "Good enough," he said. "Now, amigo, you are going to have to work on their expressions. Right now they look like starving Lithuanian refugees about to be processed into dog food by the SS. Not a cheery sight, is it?"

"Smile, kids," I said, bending to the Argus.

The kids looked dead in the viewfinder.

"*Smile* won't get it, amigo," Billetdoux said. "Smile is the kiss of death in this racket. You might as well ask them to whistle Puccini. No, you've got to bring out some personality, whether they've got any or not. You want to get something on their faces their mama will blink her eyes at in wonder. You want her to think that she's never really *seen* her own kids. Got the idea?" He knelt down in front of the kids and raised his hands up like an orchestra leader. "I want you kids to say something for Uncle Billy Ducks, will you?" The kids nodded. "I want you kids to say, 'Hanna ate the whole banana,' and I want you to say it together until Uncle Billy Ducks tells you to quit, okay?"

He stood up and said to me, "Take ten shots. Press the shutter button between 'whole' and 'banana.' Got it? Okay kids, start saying it." He raised his hands like an orchestra leader again and started the kids chanting the phrase. I hit the button too soon the first time, too late the second, but I gradually fell into the rhythm of their sing-song chant and was able to snap their pictures on the simulated smile generated when their mouths were opened wide on "whole" but starting to close for "banana."

I took ten pictures, then shut off the floods. Billetdoux was nowhere in sight. I felt uneasy about our being alone in the house with these kids. The heat of the floods had raised a greasy sweat on my back. Then Billetdoux came in. He had a pork chop in his hand.

"There's some grub in the icebox, amigo, if you're for it," he said. "Make yourself some lunch." He bit into the pork chop hungrily. "I'll say this," he said, chewing fast. "The lady of the house knows how to fry a chop."

Billetdoux began rummaging through the drawers of a built-in sideboard that filled one wall of the small living room. "Hello there," he said, lifting a pair of candle holders out of a drawer. "Take a look, amigo." He hefted the candle holders as if weighing them for value. "Solid sterling, I believe," he said. He slipped them into his jacket pocket. Then he continued rummaging. The kids didn't pay any attention to him. They were still mumbling "Hanna ate the whole banana," as they watched me taking down the floods. I worked fast, sweating not just from heat now but from fear. "Hello hello hello," Billetdoux crooned, dumping the contents of a big black purse onto the dining room table. "Coin of the old realm – silver dollars, amigo. Cartwheels. 1887. The real McCoy. The landowners here appear to be silver hoarders . . . shameful, no?" He picked up one of the silver dollars and bit it lightly. Then he shoveled the big coins into a pile and began to fill his pockets with them. "It's rotten to hoard money like this when there's so much real need in the world today," he said, his voice husky with moral outrage.

"Let's go," I said.

"One momento, por favor, kid," he said. "Nature calls." He disappeared into the back of the house. I snapped the equipment case shut, picked it up and headed for the door. I heard the sound of water hitting water followed by a toilet flushing. As I opened the front door I believed I could hear him brushing his teeth vigorously.

I waited outside, down the street. He showed up in a few minutes, his pockets bulging, another pork chop in his felonious hand. He had an electric frying pan under one arm and a desk encyclopedia under the other. "You didn't get any lunch, amigo," he said, his forehead furrowing with concern. "What's the matter, no appetite? You got a flu bug? Here, this chop is for you. You need to keep up your strength in this business."

I put the equipment case down. "You're a thief!" I said, realizing that this surge of righteousness was about ten minutes late.

He lowered the pork chop slowly. He looked astonished, then deeply hurt. "Say again, amigo? Billy Ducks a *thief*?"

"You heard me," I said, unmoved by his dismay.

"You're too harsh, amigo. I assure you it will all go toward an excellent cause. Look at it this way, try to see it as a redistribution of wealth. It's good for a society to have its wealth redistributed from time to time. Otherwise you wind up like the Egypt of the Pharaohs – a few tycoons eating chili and caviar in their plush houseboats on the Nile, and everybody else straining their milk shoving big slabs of granite around the desert. Does that make sense to you? Is this an ideal society?"

"How am I supposed to go back there with an eight-by-ten glossy of those kids?"

He raised the pork chop thoughtfully, then bit into it. "Well, amigo, you won't have to. This was just a practice run. I'll develop and print that film and see what you came up with. Consider it basic training. Boot camp. This is boot camp."

Boot camp lasted a week. Billetdoux was a good salesman. He almost always got into a house, and when he didn't, he vowed to me that he'd come back with a vengeance. I didn't ask him what he meant because I'd begun to suspect that he was crazy. I guess I would have quit after that session with the kids, but I figured that once I was out on my own his activities and mine would be separate. He was a thief, he was crazy, but I wasn't. He would develop and print my film and pay me my commissions and that would be the extent of our relationship. I wanted the job badly enough to gloss over my own objections. I liked the idea of taking pictures door to door. It was better than working in a sawmill or on a road crew or baling hay for some stingy farmer. I'd be out in nice neighborhoods every day, I'd meet interesting people, no foreman looking over my shoulder, no time clock to punch.

The last day of boot camp Billetdoux parked his car – a 1939 Chevy whose interior smelled of moss – at the edge of the most exclusive neighborhood in town, Bunker Hill Estates. "Top of the world, amigo," he said, sipping black wine from a square bottle. The neighborhood was lush and hilly, the houses sprawling and surrounded by vast, perfectly tended lawns. "The land of the Pharaohs, amigo," he said. "Makes me jumpy, going up against them. I need this little bracer." He offered the bottle to me and I took a sip. It was sweet, thick wine, like cough syrup.

We got out of the car and started walking up the steep street toward the looming estates of Bunker Hill. Billetdoux began laboring right away, wheezing, barely able to put one foot in front of the other. I was carrying all the equipment, but he acted as if he had the full load. "I don't feel so hot, amigo," he said, stopping next to a tall bushy hedge. His face had gone white, his mouth a torn pocket: The Mask of Tragedy. There was a short picket fence on the street side of the hedge. Immediately behind the fence was a narrow flower bed, then the hedge. Billetdoux stepped over the fence and into the flowers. "I'm sick," he said. He unbuckled his belt. He took off his jacket and handed it to me. He dropped his pants and squatted into the hedge until only his pale, stricken face was showing. A dark eruption of bowel noise broke the tranquil air. Billetdoux sighed. "Lord," he said. "What a relief. Must have been that goddamned chokecherry wine." He smiled weakly. I stood there, holding his jacket, the full weight of the incredible situation beginning to impress itself on me. A small dog, alerted by the commotion, came snapping up to Billetdoux. The dog was perfectly groomed. It looked like a blond wig that had come to life. Billetdoux put a hand out to it, to appease it or to

ward it off, and the dog bit his finger. Billetdoux fell backward into
the hedge, disappearing. The dog went after him, lusting for blood
after his initial success with this hedge-fouling trespasser. Then they
both emerged, Billetdoux roaring to his feet, the dog in frenzied
attack. "Son of a bitch," Billetdoux said, picking the dog up roughly
by its collar, a satiny bejeweled affair. "I hate small dogs like this,
don't you amigo? Probably eats anchovies and cake."

I looked up and down the street, expecting a crowd of curious
Bunker Hill residents attracted by the ruckus, but the street remained
empty and serene. I was in awe before that unperturbed serenity. It
was the serenity of people who knew who they were, enjoyed it, and
who believed in their basic indispensability to the great scheme of
things. Pharaohs. Serene Pharaohs untouched by the small and large
calamities that nipped at the heels of people like Billetdoux and me.

I turned back to Billetdoux. He was squatting back into the hedge,
the dog firmly in his hand. "I really hate these lap dogs," he said, "but
sometimes they come in handy."

"What are you *doing*?" I said. But I could see very well what he was
doing. He was using the small dog for toilet paper.

"It's all they're good for, dogs like these," he said, a sinister joy
playing on his lips. "Bite my jewels, you little pissant, and I'll feed you
to the flowers."

The dog whined pitifully. Billetdoux tossed it aside and stood up.
The dog burrowed into the thick hedge, making a shrill whistling
noise. "I feel much better, thanks," Billetdoux said to no one's inquiry
as he buckled up. I handed him his jacket and he slipped it on, squar-
ing his shoulders in the manner of someone who has just finished
important business and is ready for the next challenge. He stepped
over the picket fence. "Well, don't just stand there, amigo. Time, like
the man said, is money."

We continued up the street, stopping, finally, at the crest of the hill. Billetdoux leaned on a mail drop. "Look," he said, "you can see the whole town from up here. Lovely, no? See the smoke from the mills? See the pall it makes across the town's humble neighborhoods? Wouldn't it be nice to live up here where the air is pure, where all you can smell is flowers and money? What do you think, amigo? Think I should buy a house up here, with the Pharaohs?"

"Sure," I said, thinking of the ten bucks I loaned him that first day, the twenty I'd loaned him since, thinking of his wife and child, his wrecked yard, his mildewed Chevy.

He laughed bitterly. "No way, amigo. I couldn't take it. Too stuffy, if you know what I mean. A man couldn't be himself up here. I'd wind up playing their game . . . Who's Got It Best."

We walked along a narrow, tree-lined street called Pinnacle Drive. Billetdoux pointed at the street sign. "Here we are – the top of the world. The Pinnacle. Everything is downhill from here. That's the definition of *pinnacle*, isn't it? Isn't that what they're trying to tell us? You're damn straight it is."

It might have been true. The houses were two and three stories and wide as aircraft hangars. Giant blue-green lawns were fitted with precise landscaping. Three to four cars gleamed in every garage.

We stopped at the biggest house on Pinnacle Drive, a slate-gray four-story saltbox affair with a seven-foot wrought-iron fence surrounding it.

"What do you see, amigo," Billetdoux said, his voice cagey.

"A nice house."

"A nice house, he says. Look again, amigo. It's a monument, dedicated to arrogance, greed, and the status quo."

I looked again. I saw a nice house with a long sloping lawn studded with beautiful shrubs, a piece of metal sculpture – a seal or possibly a bear – curled at the base of a fine elm.

"You're stone blind," Billetdoux said when I told him this. "You'll never be a real photographer. You've got scales on your eyes. Stick to mothers and babies – don't take up real picture-taking. Promise me that, will you?"

Billetdoux stepped up onto the stone retaining wall that held the iron fence. He grabbed the bars and began to yell. "Hey! You in there! We're on to you! We smell your goddamned embalming fluid, you fat-assed Egyptian mummies!" He began to laugh, enormously entertained by his performance.

Twin Dobermans came galloping up to the fence. The drapes of the front room moved. The Dobermans leaped at the fence, going for Billetdoux's hands. "I bet they've got us covered with tommy guns," he said, stepping off the retaining wall. "Look at those front doors, amigo. Eight feet tall and wide enough to run a double column of storm troopers through them. Now tell me, do you honestly feel there is warm human activity blundering around behind those dead-bolted doors? No you don't. Tight-assed, nasty, withered old Pharaoh and his Pharaohette live in there, stinking the place up with embalming fluid. Christ, amigo, it turns my stomach." He sat down suddenly on the retaining wall and covered his face with his hands. His shoulders heaved, as if racked with sobs, but he made no sound. "Lona is sick," he said, half whispering. "That's why I steal things. You called it right, kid, I'm a thief." He looked at me, his face fighting a severe emotion that threatened to dissolve it. "These people get a head cold and they fly to the Mayo Clinic. I can't even buy medicine for Lona." He took out his handkerchief and mopped his face with it. "Give me the Argus, amigo. I'll show you how to take a picture."

I opened the equipment case and handed him the camera. He began snapping pictures of the house. The drapes of the front room moved gently as if the house were suddenly filled with soft breezes.

"I'm looking at those doors," he said, sighting through the camera. "I'm looking at the shadow that falls across them on a severe diagonal due to the overhang above the steps. The effect, amigo, is grim. Now I'm sliding over to the left to include a piece of that window. This is interesting. This is the geometry of fear – a specialty of the Egyptians." He snapped a few more pictures, then handed me the camera. "Everything makes a statement, whether it wants to or not," he said. "It's up to you, as a photographer, to see and record it – in that order. *Seeing*, amigo, that will come with maturity."

Billetdoux was full of himself. His eyes were shining with the power and accuracy of his perceptions. He looked stronger and more self-confident and even healthier than ever. He looked brave and intelligent and generous and sane. I raised the Argus and took a picture of him.

The front doors of the house opened. A tall, silver-haired man in a jumpsuit came down the steps shading his eyes to see us better. Seeing their master approach, the Dobermans renewed their attack. They leaped at the fence, turned full circles in midair, came down stiff-legged and gargling with rage.

"Down Betsy, down Arnold," said the silver-haired man when he reached us. "Is there something I can do for you gentlemen?" he asked, a charming smile on his handsome face. He was elegant and calm and genuinely undisturbed by us.

Billetdoux shoved his hand through the bars of the fence, offering it to the old man. "We're doing some free-lancing for the *Clarion*," he said. I waved the camera for proof.

"Ah, journalists," said the man, dignifying us.

"Right," Billetdoux said, grinning horribly.

"Well, why don't you come inside and take some pictures of our antiques? Nedda, my wife, is a collector."

Billetdoux looked at me, his face so deadpan that I almost giggled. We followed the old man along the fence to the main gate. He sent the dogs away and then let us in.

The man's wife, Nedda, showed us through the house. It was

tastefully furnished with antiques. The dry, musty smell of old money was everywhere. It rose up in the dust from the Oriental carpets. It fell from the handsomely papered walls. It lived in the stately light that slanted into the rooms from the tall windows. It was a friendly, bittersweet smell, like stale chocolate, or maybe like the breath of a Pharaoh.

After the tour, we were given ham sandwiches and coffee, along with cole slaw. Nedda brought a tray of wonderfully frosted cookies and refilled our coffee cups. Then we toured the house again, the fourth floor where Nedda kept her most prized antiques. Billetdoux, still playing the journalist, snapped a dozen flash pictures. He was working with a kind of controlled panic, on the verge of breaking an avaricious sweat. His jacket pocket clinked with dead flash bulbs.

Then we went downstairs, exchanged a few more pleasantries, and left. "Guess you were wrong about them," I said.

He brushed the air between us with his hand. "Petty bourgeois front, amigo. Don't kid yourself."

"What's wrong with Lona?" I asked, surprising myself.

He shrugged. "The twentieth century," he said. "It depresses her. She's very sensitive."

"Oh," I said.

"You think being depressed is a picnic?" he said, annoyed at my tone. "It's an illness, amigo, serious as cancer."

"Really," I said.

He looked at me strangely, then slapped his stomach hard. He made a loud barking sound.

"What's wrong?" I asked.

"I can't eat cole slaw. The bastards put out cole slaw." We were halfway to the front gate. "I can't make it, amigo. Let's head back." He turned quickly and headed back toward the front doors. The Dobermans didn't come after us, though I expected them to come sailing around the house at any second. Billetdoux, doubled over and barking, ran up the steps of the front porch. He rang the bell until the door opened.

"The journalists," said the pleasant old man.

"Please," Billetdoux grunted. "Can I use your facilities?"

"Most certainly," said the old man. "Do come in."

The old man led Billetdoux away. I waited in the foyer. Nedda saw me. "Oh you're back," she said.

"Yes, ma'am," I said. "My boss had to use your bathroom. He can't eat cole slaw."

She touched her cheek with her fingers. "Oh dear," she said. "I'm so sorry. I hope he isn't too distressed. Would you like some candy while you're waiting?"

"Yes, ma'am," I said. So these are the Pharaohs, I thought.

She went out and came back with a box of chocolates. I studied the brown shapes, then selected one I hoped was filled with cream instead of a hard nut.

"Oh take *more*," she said, holding the box closer to me. "Fill your pocket. I'm not allowed them anyway. Neither is Burton."

Billetdoux came in, smelling of expensive cologne. "Let's hit the road, amigo," he said. "We've bothered these fine people long enough."

"No bother at all," said Nedda. "We don't get much company these days. I'm glad you came. Do drop in again."

Out on the street Billetdoux said, "Christ, what a pair of phonies. I thought we'd never get out of there."

"Better check your wallet," I said.

He looked at me sharply but didn't say anything. I popped a chocolate into my mouth. Mint cream. I didn't offer him one. He reached into his pocket and took out a small sculpture of a Chinese monk lifting a wineskin to his grinning lips.

"Look at this piece of junk," he said. "I thought it was some kind of special jade, white jade maybe, but it's only soapstone. Chances are all those antiques are phonies, too." He tossed the guzzling monk into a shrub as we walked downhill toward his car.

After my first one-hundred-dollar week, Billetdoux invited me over to celebrate my success. "You're on your way, amigo," he said, uncapping a quart of cheap vodka. He made us a pair of iceless screwdrivers and we clinked glasses before drinking. "Here's to the hotshot," he said. "Here's to the man with the charm."

We drank half a dozen screwdrivers before we ran out of frozen orange juice. Then we switched to vodka on the rocks, minus the rocks. His mood changed as we got drunk.

"Here's to the hotdog capitalist," he said, turning ugly. "Here's to J. P. Morgan Junior."

He spread the photographs of Nedda's antiques out on the table before us. "There could be some money in these items, amigo. Enough to finance my retirement. Enough to escape the twentieth century. Unless they're fakes." He looked at me then, his eyes hard and rock steady. "How about it, amigo?"

"How about what?" I said, thick-tongued.

"How about we take it. How about we pay a midnight visit to Pinnacle Drive and get us a truckload of antiques?"

My mouth was already dry from the vodka, but it went drier. "No way," I said. "I'm a photographer, not a felon."

"Photographer my suffering ass!" he said. "You just don't have the belly for it, amigo. Look at yourself. You're about to muddy your drawers." He laughed happily, poured more vodka. My stomach rumbled on cue, and he laughed again.

Dinner was a blistered pizza that was both soggy and scorched. Shyanne made it from a kit. She cut it into eight narrow slices. Billetdoux and I ate at the kitchen table. Shyanne carried a tray into Lona's bedroom, then went into the living room with her two slices of pizza to watch TV.

"I should have gotten some T-bones," Billetdoux said.

"No, this is fine," I said.

"Don't bullshit a bullshitter, amigo," he said.

To change the subject, I told him about some of my weirder customers. I told him about the old weightlifting champ who posed for me in a jockstrap, holding a flower pot in each hand to make his biceps bulge. I told him about the couple who took turns sitting on each other's lap, touching tongues. Then there was the crackpot who wore a jungle hat and spoke German at a full shout to a photograph of his dead wife.

Billetdoux wasn't amused. "You think the human condition is a form of entertainment for us less unfortunate citizens, amigo?" he said. "Remember, 'There but for the grace of God go I.'"

I thought about this for a few seconds. "Sometimes it is," I said, refusing to buckle under to his hypocritical self-righteousness. "Sometimes it's entertaining as hell."

He glowered at me, then brightened. "Hey, come out to the garage with me. I want to show you something."

I stood up, felt the floor tilt and rotate, sat back down. When the room stabilized itself, I got up again.

Outside, the air was crisp. A cold wind seemed to be falling straight down out of the sky. Billetdoux opened the garage door and switched on the lights. "Ta da!" he sang.

A long pearl-gray car gleamed in the overhead light. "Wow," I said, honestly moved. "What is it?"

"That is a *car*, amigo," he said. "It's a 1941 LaSalle. I got it for a song from an old lady who didn't know what she had. It's been in storage – only eleven thousand miles on it."

We got in. The interior was soft, dark gray plush. Even the door, when it latched, sounded like money slapping money. Billetdoux started it and backed out onto his lawn.

"It's a little dusty," he said, getting out of the car. "I'm going to hose it off. Dust will murder a finish like this."

I went back into the house. I found the vodka and poured some into my glass. Noise, like a mob of crows in flight, passed through the kitchen. I looked out the kitchen window. Billetdoux was leaning against the front fender of the LaSalle. He saw me and winked. He began to undulate, as if performing sex with the car. "I think I'm in love," he shouted.

What sounded like a mob of raucous crows was actually Lona. She was singing in a language that might have been Egyptian. She could have been strumming her guitar with a trowel for all the music that was coming out of it. Then a tremendous crash shook the house. Glass tinkled.

Billetdoux came in. "Are they at it again?" he asked me. Glass shattered. Wood splintered. "Oh oh," he said.

Oh oh seemed like a totally failed response to the din.

Billetdoux sighed weakly. "I smell trouble," he said.

We poured ourselves some vodka. The uproar changed in character. Two voices were now harmonizing in throat-tearing screams. Now and then something made the walls shake.

"Maybe we'd better have us a look," he said, sipping.

I sipped too. Outside the kitchen window, the perfect LaSalle gleamed like a classy rebuttal to human life.

We went to the back of the house. Lona's bedroom door was open. For a second or two I didn't understand what I was looking at. What I saw was Lona and Shyanne kneeling face to face on the bed, combing each other's hair. A dresser was lying on its side and a mirror was on the floor cracked diagonally in half. I saw, then, that neither one of them had combs in their hands. Just great knots of hair. Lona was growling through her clenched teeth and Shyanne was *hissing*. Shyanne's mouth was very wide and the teeth were exposed. She looked like a cheetah. Then they fell over and rolled to the floor. They rolled toward us and we stepped back, holding our drinks high. The air before us was filled with flailing legs and whipping hair. "Knock it off, okay?" Billetdoux suggested meekly. He watched them a while longer, then set his drink on the floor. "Give me a hand, will you, amigo?" he said.

He grabbed Shyanne under the armpits and lifted her off Lona. She continued to kick out at Lona as Billetdoux pulled her into the hall. I reached for a waving leg, then thought better of it. Lona got heavily to her feet. Her gray hair had shapes wrung into it. Horns, knobs, antennas. Lumps that suggested awful growths. She picked up a lamp and flung it at Shyanne, who was no longer in the room. It exploded against the wall, next to my head. "God damn you to hell," she said to me, but meaning, I think, Shyanne.

"Fat witch! Pus hole! Slop ass!" Shyanne yelled from somewhere else in the house.

After things quieted down, Billetdoux fixed us a new round of drinks. Vodka and warm apricot nectar. "That was intensely embarrassing, amigo," he said. "They go ape shit about once a month or so. Don't ask me why."

I made some kind of suave gesture indicating the futility of things in general, but it didn't come off well since I was barely eighteen and hadn't yet earned the right to such bleak notions. I pulled in my gesturing hand so that it could cover my mouth while I faked a coughing fit.

But Billetdoux wasn't paying any attention to me. "The television, the guitar," he said. "This house is too small for us. They tend to get on each other's nerves. Sometimes it comes to this."

I was drunk enough to say, "How come you let your daughter treat her mother that way?"

Billetdoux looked at me. "My daughter?" he said. "What are you saying, amigo?"

"Your daughter, Shyanne, she . . ."

"My *daughter*? You think I'm beyond insult, amigo? You think we've reached a point in time where anything at all can be said to Price Billetdoux?" For the first time he pronounced his name in accurate French.

"She's *not* your daughter?" I said, thoroughly numb to the hard-edged peculiarities of Billetdoux's life, but somewhat surprised anyway.

"*Damn*," he said, glumly.

"Then Lona . . ."

"Lona? Lona? Jesus, amigo, what godawful thing are you going to say now?"

"I thought Lona was your wife."

"Lona," he said, measuring his words, "is my mom." His voice was dark with a dangerous reverence that adjusted my frame of mind for the rest of the evening.

Shyanne came into the kitchen. She opened the fridge and took out a bottle of Upper Ten. She made a face at Billetdoux, then at me. "Oh baby baby," Billetdoux said, his voice wounded with love.

"I think you should tell her to move out," Shyanne said.

"Oh, baby. No. You know I can't do that. It would kill her."

"How do you think *I* feel?" she said. "Maybe you want *me* to move out. Is that what you want?" Her small red lips puckered into a hard toy-doll pout. "I'll *go*. I'll just *go*."

"Don't say that, baby," Billetdoux said, miserably.

Shyanne still looked twelve years old to me. But the hard unwavering stare she had leveled at me was not something a child was capable of. I moved her age up to sixteen or seventeen. But something older by five thousand years hung stupidly in her face.

"Say the word, I'll go. I'll pack," she said.

I went out into the front room as Billetdoux began to weep on the small breast of his teenage wife.

I switched the TV to *The Perry Como Show*. I watched it all. Then I switched to *Wagon Train*. I had ignored the sounds coming from the kitchen – the soft, singsong assurances, the cooing words that dissolved into groaning embraces, the serious oath-making, the baby-talk threats, and, finally, the mindless chitchat.

Billetdoux came in and sat down on the couch next to me. He was eating a peanut butter sandwich and drinking beer. "What can I say, amigo?" he said. "Are you going to think of me now as an old cradle robber? Hell, I'm only thirty-eight. Shyanne's almost sixteen. You think that's too young?"

I shrugged. "What's a dozen years more or less," I said, my arithmetic deliberately sentimental.

He straightened up, set his sandwich and beer down on the coffee table. "My situation is not easy, amigo. I'm so crazy about Shyanne. I can't live without her. You understand? No, you don't. Maybe someday you will, if you get lucky. At the same time, I've got to think about Lona. I can't set her adrift after all she's done for me, can I?"

"No," I said, remembering to be careful.

Billetdoux was chewing his lower lip and absentmindedly cracking his knuckles. "Mom thinks the world of me," he said. "Did I tell you that? She calls me her Honey Boy."

I went back to the kitchen to get myself an Upper Ten. My stomach felt like I'd swallowed a cat. Shyanne was still at the table. She was looking at her hands, studying first the tops, then the bottoms.

"They're red," she said, without looking up. "I hate these hands. Look at them. They're not very elegant, are they?"

I got my Upper Ten, opened it.

"I'm sick of my hands," she said. "I'd just as soon cut them off."

She tried to show me her hands, but I walked past them and back to the living room. Billetdoux was pacing in front of the TV. "I'm going to Carnuba the LaSalle," he said. "It's been on my mind." He stalked out, like a man with pressing business.

I sipped my pop. Some kind of detective show was on now. After a while, Shyanne came in and sat next to me. Lona was strumming her guitar again and singing in Egyptian. "Are you going to take me fishing or not?" Shyanne said, her lips brushing my ear. Her tone of voice made me feel as though I'd broken every promise I'd ever made.

"Did I say I would?" I said.

"No one's taken me fishing since we came to this dumb town."

I noticed she was sitting on her hands.

"I know what you're thinking," she said, turning her face sidelong to mine. "I know *exactly* what you're thinking."

I got up and went outside. Billetdoux was out on the lawn rubbing wax into the gleaming LaSalle. He was holding a flashlight in one hand and buffing with the other. "Amigo," he said. "Loan me twenty before you go, okay? I'm in a bit of a jam."

I gave him twenty without comment and walked away. I felt, then, that I'd seen enough of the Billetdoux family and that I wouldn't be back, ever.

But half an hour later I was in his kitchen again for no reason other than a vaguely erotic curiosity. I made myself another vodka and nectar and took it out to the backyard. It was a clear, moonless night. *The moon*, I thought, *is in Egypt.*

I sat on the dead grass and drank until I got sick. The sickness was sudden and total and my stomach emptied itself colossally into the lawn. When I was able to sit up again, I saw Lona. She was standing before the open bedroom window, naked, her strangely tranquil face upturned to the sky. Her eyes were closed and she was holding her arms out in front of her, palms up, in a gesture that reminded me of ancient priestesses. Her big silver breasts gleamed in the chilly starlight.

"Honey Boy," she said, her eyes still closed, her face still raised to the delicate radiations of the night. "Honey Boy, come here."

I got up heavily. I thoroughly believed in that moment that I had once again decided to leave. But I found myself walking trancelike to *Lona*. Like an inductee to a great and lofty sect, having passed my preliminary ordeal, I moved, awestruck, as if toward the sphinx.

David Graham. *Route 15,*
Gettysburg, PA, 1986. Type C
print. (Courtesy the photographer.
Copyright © 1986 David Graham)

Highspeed Linear Main St.

H O B   B R O U N

The darkroom is a good place to work on my theory that electrons move faster as you travel south toward the Equator. Four rolls of Tri-X are turning slowly in developer, part of the project out of which my tangent theory came like a bee from the hive. Am I going too fast?

I meant to track on film and in words, improvisationally, the New York–Key West highway experience. Note the verb tense. Germ idea and what it becomes through process should be discrete.

Already you will be wanting context. Fair enough. I am a man in early middle age, precise to a fault in my habits, but given no less to loose talk. My marriage is nine years old. I am lugubrious; Daphne is the one with the fizz. She likes me to threaten her over the phone. I am happy to do this.

The serial windshield narrative makes lists.

Wigwam Village	molded fiberglass colossi	Caves of Mystery
auto bazaar	Big Boy	Tile Town
dinosaur park	Tower of Pizza	chalet motel
Toto's	Zeppelin Diner	drive-thru bank

I know that tempo is important and I constantly watch the clock. Looking a magazine over, I calculate how many minutes it will take to read this or that article. Normally, I will have the TV on as well and possibly be talking on the phone. Daphne says, unfairly, that I'm afraid to sit still and concentrate. But I am well-known for hand-tinted still-life arrangements.

Modus operandi: montage, collage, bricolage.

scratch 'n' sniff stickers
fruit-shaped gumballs
rubber animals
copper jewelry
pocket guides
budget tapes
cedar boxes
pennants
ashtrays
keyrings
posters
decals

Art is a business, but not so the reverse. I talk on the phone, have lunch, that's it. I don't sleep with curators.

On the phone to Daphne, I speak in a natural voice.

"Believe it. Frankie knows how to put edge on a knife. Thin oil and a smooth stone."

I often call from the booth in the Ramayana while my koftas, dal, and chapatis are being prepared. This booth is right next to the kitchen; its aromas inspire me. Later, when I'm having coffee, Preva or Subash, one of the brothers, will sit down with me to talk. They share my Salem Lights and ask me to clarify words. Recently, the brothers have invested in a record label. "Picture wallah," one of them will say. "We are confused by 'rock the house.'" I try to caution them, but they will not be cautioned. The label, dealing in rap music only, has offices in Jersey City.

Painting has destroyed "landscape," and left us with "map."

Trenton	onion rings
Havre de Grace	crabcakes
Virginia Beach	sausage po'boy
Greenville	chess pie
Savannah	drop biscuits
Opa-Locka	moros y cristianos

I like to draw parallels. Daphne calls this "laying track." I reply that converging rails teach perspective to small children. Perhaps, Daphne says, this is why as adults their definitions blur. Stella, our daughter, is six and takes no side.

"I'm *sooo* exhausted," she says, collapsing theatrically at our feet.

But of course, right there, by posing she makes a parallel, an alter ego.

Daphne says, "Mimicry is not analogy."

Yes, we are being insufferable. Lunch resumes with humorless laughter; the salad dressing features basil from our window box, the coffee is brewed very dark.

"Stella! Will you come out from under the table?"

"Just as a for instance," I begin. My wife chews grimly. Are these the glinting eyes I fell in love with? "Just as a for instance, isn't it amazing that at one time in Ireland they bled their cows to mix with milk just as the Masai do in Kenya today?"

"No."

When Daphne has the last word, it is usually of one syllable.

park-way *n. a broad roadway bordered by trees and shrubs. (soften curves, plantings to guard from dazzle and wind, harmonize design)*
free-way *n. a multi-lane divided highway with fully controlled access. (eliminate curves, invite glare, engineer velocity)*

One idea was, What would Frankie see? How would he react? Would Frankie on the road be restless or deliberate? With a ballpoint

I wrote L-O-V-E on the knuckles of my left hand and H-A-T-E on the right, but it wasn't the answer. Eye-level compositions were not the answer. Should I try not to focus at all?

Increasingly, my sensible Datsun was an embarrassment, a timid signature. Frankie would drive some kind of muscle car with tachometer, Frenched headlights, a hood scoop. I pictured an expanse of tailfin in thirty coats of hand-rubbed candy-apple red. I thought of the acute angle as an abstraction of speed, thrust, dynamism. What is it to understand a language and still not be able to speak it?

ALBERT FRANCONA

AKA "Frankie"
White Male
Age: 29
Height: 5'10"
Weight: 160
Color of Eyes: Black
Color of Hair: Black

SUBJECT IS WANTED IN CONNECTION WITH SERIES OF
AGGRAVATED SEXUAL ASSAULTS IN NEW ENGLAND AND
MID-ATLANTIC STATES. KNOWN TO FREQUENT PHOTO
STUDIOS, GREASE PITS, BOWL-A-RAMAS. SCORNS FIREARMS,
BUT SHOULD BE CONSIDERED EXTREMELY DANGEROUS.

It takes vigilance not to succumb to the numbers – f-stops, motel rates, highway designations, diner checks, exposure times – and one is not always up to it. The odometer turning to 50,000 becomes an anticipated Event. The glove compartment fills up with receipts, a wealth of documentation. Billboards and license plates turn unpreventably into algebra. A certain fecklessness sets in. And then a certain tension, which can be relieved only by sight of time and temperature specified in filament bulb mosaic on the rotating sign in front of a small-town bank.

Awareness deluges when not modulated, when not finely tuned. It can become a kind of panic.

Expenditure: $62.31

1,738 miles @ 26 mpg

67 gals. gas @ avg. price 93 cents

Stella, legally, should be starting school, but my wife and I are loath to part with her. Is this a lack of faith in institutions, or something more selfish? Either way, it probably is natural for members of the overeducated class. Daphne's mother cannot say often enough that her daughter is "too clever by half." In my own case, form follows function until exhausted but never catches up. A rerun in every direction, I mean. Stella announces: "Chocolate is fabulous." Daphne has on Verdi or Bizet, and Stella shudders, yells, "I hate this music!" She has something to say with these words; they are not merely thrown up like tinsel onto a tree. We cherish in her such certainties, such firm insistence, and are loath to see them replaced by anxiety, ambivalence, embarrassment, retreat – what, in short, seem to be the necessary perversions.

ROADWAY VERNACULAR
(A Preliminary Syllabus)

Baines, Melissa, *Urban Motif Congestion*, Argon Press, West Covina, 1979.

De Marco, H. D., *Rest and Respite: From Caravanserai to Truckstop*, printed privately, 1968.

McMahon, T. K., *Looking at the World Through a Windshield*, HomeRun Books, San Francisco, 1981.

Niemann, Dieter, *Phänomenologie des Autobahns*, Kultur Zeitung, Bern, 1977.

Platt, David Alan, *Neon Democracy*, Dreyfuss-Peterkin, Boston, 1983.

Traven, Bob, *First with the Best: A History of U.S. 1*, Tire & Rubber Institute, Akron, 1965.

"Don't get too wrapped up," said nearly everyone who knew about my project. "Drive safely."

I carried in the trunk of my car a first-aid kit, jumper cables, flares, a heavy-duty flashlight, kept my thermos filled with coffee, was careful to husband my energies and stay alert. Still, as it turned out, the dice weren't sufficiently loaded.

I remember a distinct but unnamable shift of light, hard impact, raining glass, and then a kind of torpid, nauseous remove that was almost like snobbery. "Oh, just relax," I might have said. Or, "Call the roller of big cigars." I remember a texture of white clamshell, surf hissing around my ears. And O'Hara, unmarked and unfazed, the prick, his Dodge half-ton barely scraped, O'Hara making a cozy offer, his arm around me, snuff-stained teeth and rapid blinking.

In the taxi, I came more to myself, lenses spread out around me on the seat. Blue sea and blue sky seemed to roll as one. Just the note, I thought, to fill and then combine the chord. Go on. Make friends with it.

I sold the car and flew home.

DAY OF ACCIDENT May 18, 1986	
TIME OF DAY	10:15 A.M.
WEATHER	Clear
LIGHT CONDITION	Daylight
ROAD SURFACE	Dry
OCCURRED ON (Name St., Rd. or Rte. #)	U.S. 1
AT INTERSECTION WITH (Name St., Rd. or Rte. #)	Dade Co. 905
CITY NAME (Or Nearest City)	Key Largo

I look over the four contact sheets while they are still wet, am pleased right off to see a balance of formal and informal, a mixture of broad long-shot and close-in detail. I pour out another glass of Old

Overholt, straight rye whiskey bottled in Cincinnati, and, along with my big-band tapes, a habitual darkroom accoutrement. True, I like certain things to be just so, but who cares any more about workmanship? These are bits, blips, snippets, and not as careful as they look. Starting anywhere. Taking the last sheet, reading the rightmost negative strip, which on its upper edge says KODAK SAFETY FILM 5063, and on its lower edge names exposures 16 through 21.

- paired gas pumps, rectangular digital display units topped with identical PAY FIRST signboards
- old man forcing smile in motel breezeway, NAPA cap, bill stained
- industrial exhaust stacks, low angle
- church steeple paralleled by traffic light stanchion
- self-portrait behind the wheel (camera held at arm's length), visible fatigue, characteristic alternation of aimless and frantic
- family group at Tastee Freez picnic table, night (flash fill)

Mom, dad, two girls, one boy. "We're a service family." Contemplative dad sipping thick shake. "MacDill AFB, Tampa. Antiaircraft. It's all computers now." Taking their latest transfer in stride, fatalists. "Work's always there, so you follow it." I had to envy resignation chosen and not settled for. Watched them roll slowly away in a camper lashed with luggage and bikes.

This is "Prelude to a Kiss." Benny Carter's 1942 band, very mellow reeds. And these still are only scraps, chips, slivers. That they can be fixed in a coherent sum is the kind of stance we live on, like entropy or antimatter: pretty fictions that don't explain, furtive agreements of pretense, a wink and a ducking away.

Modulate.

Modulate. All right.

But I can't stop wanting to know what I'm looking at.

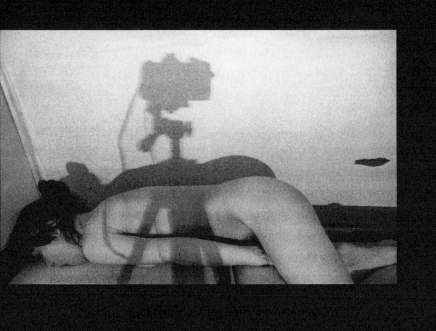

Negatives

E. A N N I E   P R O U L X

Year after year rich people moved into the mountains and built glass houses at high elevations; at sunset when the valleys were smothered in leathery shadow, the heliodor mansions flashed like an armada signaling for the attack. The newest of these aeries belonged to Buck B., a forcibly retired television personality attracted to scenery. A crew of outside carpenters arrived in the fall and labored until spring. Trucks bearing great sheets of tempered glass crept over the dirt roads. The owner stayed scarce until June when his dusty Mercedes, with an inverted bicycle on the roof, pulled up at the village store and in came Buck B. clenching a map and asking for directions to his own house.

A few weeks later the first yellow cab ever seen in the town disgorged Walter Welter in the same place. Walter, who had come a long way in ten years from Coma, Texas, called Buck B. on the pay phone, said he was at the store and Buck B. could just get down there and pick him up. The cab driver bought a can of pineapple juice and a generic cheese sandwich, waited in his taxi.

"I give 'em a year," said the storekeeper peering out between advertising placards, watching Walter transfer tripods, portfolios, cameras and six suitcases from the taxi to the Mercedes.

"Tell you what *I'd* give 'em," said the tough customer. "What *I'd* do."

But it all was all over before the first snow and no one had to do a thing.

———

"Why do you let that slut come here?" said Buck, casting his lightless eyes on Walter, who knelt beside the tub in the downstairs bathroom. Buck's hands were crusted with clay, held stiff in front of his black apron. Walter's hands were in yellow rubber gloves, scrubbing away Albina Muth's greasy ring. Buck's face was all chops and long teeth like the face of Fernandel in old French comedies; his hair rippled like silver water.

"You think you're going to get some photographs, don't you? That she's some kind of a subject. The Rural Downtrodden. And then what, the pictures lie around in stacks. Nobody but you knows what they are. The edge of an ear. A dirty foot. You better keep her out of the upstairs." He waited but Walter said nothing. After ten or eleven seconds Buck kicked the bathroom door shut, stalked back to his clay, hands held in front of him like ceremonial knives shaped for cutting out viscera.

The fingers on both hands wouldn't count the dinners Walter Welter ruined with his stories of Albina Muth. Friends came up from the city for a mountain weekend, had to listen to grisly accounts: she had left her awful husband for a deranged survivalist who hid knives under tin cans in the woods; she lived with an elderly curtain-rod salesman made such a satyr by rural retirement that Albina had been rushed twice to the emergency room; she was being prosecuted for welfare fraud; her children had head lice; she sported a vestigial tail.

They saw her at the mall supermarket standing in line with children clustered on the cart like flies, or carrying bags of beer and potato chips out to a pickup truck in the parking lot. Her children, with thick-lidded eyes and reptilian mouths, sat in the bark-strewn truck bed rolling empty soda cans. Albina, her hair squashed against her head, climbed into the passenger seat of the cab, smoked cigarettes, waiting for someone who would come later.

———

One day Walter passed her walking on the muddy shoulder of the road, the children stumbling and squalling behind her. He pulled up, asked if she wanted a ride.

"Sure as hell do." Smoky, rough voice. She stuffed the kids with their chapped, smeared faces into the back seat and got in beside him. She was thin, about the size of a twelve-year-old. Her coarse hair looked like she cut it herself with a jackknife, her white face like a folded slice of store bread. He noticed, not the color of her eyes, but the bruised-looking flesh around them.

"Know where the Bullgut Road is? Next one after that's my road. You'n drop us there." The tone was bold. She bit at her nails, spitting fragments off the tip of her tongue.

The road was a skidder-gouged track. She pulled the half-asleep children out like sacks, saying, "come on, come on," and started up through the mud, one brat jammed onto her hip, the other two coming at their own pace and crying. He waved, but she didn't look around.

At dinner he did an imitation of the way she wiped her nose on the back of her hand. Buck B. listened, tarnished hair clouded with clay dust, eating his dish of yogurt and nuts, gazing through the glass wall at the mountain. He said, "God, that's beautiful. Why don't you do mountain studies? Why don't you take pictures of something attractive?" Then he said he was afraid that Albina Muth's children had sowed the back seat of the Mercedes with louse nits. They were starting to fight when the phone rang and Walter got the last word, saying, "I'm not here if it's one of your stupid friends wanting a tree picture." He meant Barb Cigar, who once had called to say that her trees were covered with lovely perfect leaves and didn't Walter want to come with his camera? No, he did not. It was Barb Cigar with the dewlapped mouth like the flews of a hound who had given Buck B. an antique sabre reputed to have fallen from Casimir Pulaski's hand in the battle for Savannah (a parting token from her ex-father-in-law from his cutlery collection), she who had sent a youth in a panda bear suit to sing Happy Birthday under Buck's window, she who named her Rottweiler puppy "Mr. B."

Walter Welter's photographs were choked down and spare, out-of-focus, the horizons tilted, unrecognizable objects looming in the foreground, the heads of people quartered and halved. What he called the best one showed a small, boxy house with a grape arbor and a porch glider. The grass needed cutting. Guests sorting through the photographs kept coming back to this dull scene until gradually the image of the house showed its secret hostility, the arbor turned harsh and offensive, the heavy grass bent with rage. The strength of the photograph emerged as though the viewer's eye was itself a developing medium. It would happen a lot faster, said Buck, if Walter wrote out the caption: *The House where Ernest and Lora Cool were Bludgeoned by their Son, Buxton Cool.*

"If you have to say what something's about," said Walter, "it's not about anything except you saying it's about something."

"Spare me," said Buck, "spare me these deep philosophical insights."

Walter's photographer friends sent him prints: an arrangement of goat intestines on backlit glass, a dead wallaby in a water hole, a man – chin up – swallowing a squid tentacle coming out of a burning escalator, Muslim women swathed in curtains of blood. One of the friends called from Toronto, said he'd spent the summer with the archeologists flying over the north looking for tent rings. "There was this Inuit cache on the Boothia Peninsula." Distance twisted his voice into a thinning ribbon.

The wooden box, he said, fell apart when it was lifted from the earth. Inside they had found knives, scrapers, two intact phonograph records of religious music, a bullet mold, a pair of cracked spectacles, a cooking pot stamped REO, needles, a tobacco can. From the tobacco can they took a dozen negatives, the emulsion cracked with age. Prints were on the way to Walter.

When they arrived he was disappointed. All but one of the photographs showed squinting missionaries. The other photograph was of an Inuit child in front of a weather-whitened building. Her anorak was sewn in a pattern of chevrons and in the crazed distance lay a masted ship. Her face had the shape of a hazelnut, the eyebrows curved like willow leaves. She leaned against the scarred clapboards, arms folded over her breast, mouth set in a pinched smile and both eyes lost in their sockets.

Walter caught the flaw in the shadow. Light coursed through the space between the soles of the child's boots and the ground because her weight was on her heels. She was propped against the building.

"It's a corpse," said Walter, delighted. "She's stiff."

Buck, toasting oatcakes, wondered what the photograph meant. "Like Nanook of the North, maybe? Starved to death? Or tuberculosis? Something like that?"

Walter said there was no point in trying to understand what it meant. "It can't mean anything to us. It only meant something to the one who put this negative in the tobacco can."

Buck, wearing a scratchy wool sweater next to his skin, said something under his breath.

Once or twice a week they drove to the mall with its chain stores, pizza stands, liquor store, sixty-minute photo shop, While-U-Wait optician, House of Shoes, bargain carpet, and Universal Herbals.

"I told you to bring the other credit card," said Buck. "I told you the Visa was ruined when it fell under the seat and you moved it back."

Walter pawed through his pockets. He leaped when Albina Muth rapped on the passenger window with a beer bottle. She was smiling, leaning out of a garbage truck parked beside them, smoke flooding out of her mouth, her rough brown hair like fur. She was wearing the same grimy, stretched-out acrylic sweater.

"Nice truck," cried Walter. "Big."

"It ain't mine. It's a friend of mine's. I'm just waitin' for him." She glanced across the highway where there were three low-slung bars: the 74, the Horseshoe, Skippy's.

Walter joked with her. In the driver's seat Buck invisibly knotted up, yanked himself into a swarm of feelings. He had found the other credit card in his own pocket. Albina threw back her head to swallow beer and Walter noticed the grainy rings of dirt on her throat.

"You take pictures?"

"Yeah."

"Well, sometime maybe you'n take one of me?"

"For god's sake," hissed Buck, "let's go."

But Walter did want to photograph her, the way she had looked that day by the side of the road, the light strong and flickering.

In October Albina Muth started to sleep in the Mercedes. Walter went out on Sunday to get the papers. There she was, so cold she couldn't sit up. He had to pull her upright. Dull, black-circled eyes, shivering fits. She couldn't say what she was doing there. He guessed it was a case of Saturday night drinking and fighting, run off and hide in somebody's car. It was a two-mile walk from the main road to somebody's Mercedes, and all in the dark.

He brought her into the house. The south wall, glass from roof to ground, framed the mountain, an ascending mass of rock in dull strokes of rose madder, brown, tongues of fume twisting out of the springs on its flanks. The mountain pressed into the room with an insinuation of augury. Flashing particles of ice dust stippled the air around the house. The wind shook the walls and liquid shuddered in the glass.

In that meaningful house Albina Muth was terrible, pallid face marked by the weave of the automobile upholstery, hands like roots, and stinking ragbag clothes. She followed Walter into the kitchen where Buck worked a mathematical puzzle and drank seaweed tea, his lowered eyelids as smooth as porcelain, one bare monk's foot tapping air.

"What?" he said, shooting up like an umbrella, jangling the cup, slopping the puzzle page. He limped from the room, the cast on his right foot tapping.

"What happened to him?" said Albina. She was attracted to sores.

Walter poured coffee. "He hit a deer."

"Didn't hurt the car none!"

"He wasn't in the car. He was riding his bicycle."

Albina laughed through a mouthful of coffee. "Hit a deer ridin' a bike!"

"The deer stood there and he thought it would run off so he kept on going but it didn't and he hit it. Then the deer did run off and Buck had a broken ankle and a wrecked bike."

She wiped her mouth, looked around. "This is some place," she said. "Not yours, though. His."

"Yeah."

"Must be rich."

"He used to be on television. Long ago. Back in the long ago. A kid's show – *Mr. B.'s Playhouse*. Before you were born. Now he makes pottery. That's one of his cups you're drinking from. That bowl with the apples."

She put her head on one side and looked at the table, the clay floor tiles, the cast-iron bulldog, the hand-carved cactus coat rack, drank the coffee with a noise like a drain and over the rim of the blue cup she winked at Walter.

"He's rich," she said. "Can I take a bath?"

What would she say, thought Walter, if she saw Buck B.'s bathroom upstairs with the François Lalanne tub in the shape of a blue hippopotamus? He showed her to the downstairs bath.

She came many times after that, walking up the private road in the dark, crawling into the car and filling it with her stale breath. Walter threw a sleeping bag in the back seat. She added a plastic trash bag stuffed with pilled sweaters and wrinkled polyester slacks, a matted hairbrush, pair of pink plastic shoes with a butterfly design punched over the toe. He wondered what she had done with her children but didn't ask.

In the mornings she waited outside the kitchen door until Walter let her in. He watched her dunk toast crusts, listened to her circular talk that collapsed inward as a seashell narrows and twists upon itself, and at noon when the bars opened he took her to the mall.

"Come on, take my picture. Nobody never took my picture since I was a kid," she said.

"Someday."

"Walter, she is living in my car," said Buck B. He could barely speak.

Walter threw him a high smile.

The deep autumn came quickly. Abandoned cats and dogs skulked along the roads. The flare of leaves died, the mountain moulted into gray-brown like a dull bird. A mood of destruction erupted when a bull got loose at the cattle auction house and trampled an elderly farmer, when a car was forced off the road by pimpled troublemakers throwing pumpkins. Hunters came for the deer and blood trickled along their truck fenders. Walter took pictures of them leaning against their pickups. Through binoculars Buck watched loggers clearcut the mountain's slope, and Albina Muth slept in the Mercedes every night.

Walter liked the road called Mud Pitch and drove past the wreck of the old poorhouse two or three times a week. This time it showed itself to him like some kind of grainy Russian nude tinted egg-yolk yellow. As he stared the sunlight failed and once more it became a ruined building. He thought he would photograph the place. Tomorrow. Or the day after.

A cold front rolled in while they slept and in the morning the light jangled through cracking clouds, the sky between the house and the mountain filled with loops of wind. The camera strap sawed into the side of Walter's neck as he ran down the terraces to the car. He could hear the bulldozers on the mountain. Albina Muth was curled up on the back seat.

"I'm working today. Got to drop you off early."

The mountain mottled and darkened under cloud shadow. There was no color in the fields, only a few deep scribbles of madder and chalky biscuit. Albina sat up, face thickened with sleep.

"I'nt bother you. Just lay here in the car. I'm sick."

"Look. I'm going to be working all day. The car will be cold."

"Can't go back up to the trailer, see? Can't go to the mall. He's there, see?"

"Don't tell me anything about it." He cut the Mercedes too far back, put the rear wheels in Buck's spider lily beds. "Don't tell me about your fights."

The poorhouse was a rack of wind-scraped buildings in fitful sunlight, glaring and then dark like the stuttering end of a reel of film spitting out numbers and raw light. Albina followed him through the burdocks.

"I thought you wanted to stay in the car and sleep."

"Oh, I'n look around."

Inside the rooms were as small as pantries and closets. Furrows of clay-colored plaster had fallen away from the lath, glass spindled across the floor. The stairs were slides of rubbish, bottles, feathers, rags.

"You gonna fix this place up?" she said kicking nut husks, pulling light chains connected to burst bulbs.

"I'm taking pictures," said Walter.

"Hey, take my picture, o.k.?"

He ignored her, went into a room: punched-out door panels, drifts of flies in the corners and the paint cracked like dried mud. He heard her in another room, scratching in the filth.

"Come in here. Stand by the window," he called. He was astonished by the complexity of light in the small chamber; a wave of abrasive gray fell in from the window, faded and deepened along the wall with the swell and heave of damp plaster. She put her arm along the top of the low window, embracing the paintless frame and resting her head on her shoulder.

"Just like that."

The light flattened so she appeared part of the window casing.

"For god's sake take that disgusting sweater off."

Her knowing smirk disappeared into the hollow of the rising sweater. She thought she knew what they were about. Her mouth ruched, she stood on alternate feet and kicked off her pants. She was all vertical, downward line, narrow arms and legs like wood strips, one nipple blank, erased by light, the other a tiny gleam in the meagre shadow of her body. She waited for Walter to bite her arms or shove her against the soiled wall. He ordered her to move around the room.

"Now by the door – put your hand on the doorknob."

Her purpled fingers half closed on the china globe. The dumb flesh took the light from the window, she coughed, leaned against the door and the paint fell in brittle flakes. But there was a doggishness about her bent shoulders, her knuckled back, that goaded him.

"Behind the door. Squeeze into that broken panel. Don't smile."

Her face appeared in the splintered opening, washed with the false importance the camera inflicts. *Click . . . whirr*

Walter's thrusting look swept the room across the hall; he saw on the floor a mound of broken glass, splinters and curved blades sloped in a truncated cone. Light pierced a broken shutter.

"Squat down over that pile of glass." A hot feeling rushed through him. It was going to be a tremendous image. He knew it.

"Jesus, I could get cut."

"You won't. Just keep your balance."

Submissively she lowered herself over the glass, the tense, bitten fingers touching the dirty floor for balance. Spots of sunlight flew across her face and neck as the clouds twitched along. She filled the viewfinder.

Again the angled limbs, the hairy shadows and glimmering flexures of her body.

"Can I put my clothes on? I'm freezin'."

"Not yet. A few more."

"Must of taken a hunderd," she cried.

"Come on."

She followed to the end of the poorhouse where green shelves pulled away, to the fallen door that led like a ramp into the world. He headed for an old kitchen stove with a water reservoir, rusting in the weeds. The oven door fell away when he grasped the handle. Albina hung back, contracted and shivering.

"Albina, pretend you're crawling into the oven."

"I want to git my clothes on."

"Right after this one. This is the last one."

"I'n wait for you in the car."

"Albina. You pestered me over and over to take your picture. Now I'm taking it. Come on, crawl into the oven."

She came through the weeds and bent before the iron hole. Her hands, her head and shoulders went into the stove's interior.

"Get in as far as you can."

The blackened, curved soles of her feet, the taut buttocks and hams, the furred pinch of sex appeared in the viewfinder. There was no vestigial tail. She began to back out as he worked the shutter.

"I wanted you to take pictures of me smilin'," she said. "Thought they was goin' to be cute, I could get like a little gold frame. Or maybe like sexy, I could put them in a little black foldup. Not gettin' in no stove, behind stickin' out."

"Albina, honey, they are cute, and some are sexy. Just a few more. Come on, stand in the hot-water thing on the side there."

She climbed up onto the stove top, saying something he couldn't hear, stepped into the water reservoir. In a cloud of rust her feet plunged through the rotten metal. The top of the range was even with her waist, and she looked as though she were to be immolated in some terrible rite. Blood ran down her foot.

Helpless, dirty laughter spurted out of the corners of his mouth and Albina wept and cursed him. But yes, now he could squeeze that hard, thin thigh, pinch the nipples until she gasped. He thrust her against the stove. Later, when he dropped her at the bar, he gave her two twenties, told her not to sleep in the car any more. She said nothing, stuffed the money in her purse and got out, walked away, the plastic bag of clothes bumping against her leg.

Milky light spilled out of the house. Buck's shadow was limping back and forth, bending down, lifting, its shape distorted by runneling moisture on the windows. Walter went in through the side door, down the back stairs to the basement darkroom.

The film creaked as he wound it onto the reel. He shook the

developing tank, stood in the sour dark listening to the slip and fall of water, watching the radiant hand of the clock. The listless water slid away, he turned on the light. Upstairs Buck walked back and forth. Walter squinted at the wet negatives, at the white pinched eyes and burning lips, the black flesh with its vacant shadows, yes, a thin arm crooked down, splayed fingers and the cone of glass that looked like smoldering coals. He really had something this time. He went upstairs.

Buck stood against the wall, hands behind his back. On his good foot he wore a brown oxford with a thick sole. There were all of Walter's suitcases at the door.

"It's getting too cold," Buck B. said, voice like a ratchet clicking through the stops.

"Too cold?"

"Too cold for staying here. I'm closing the house up. Tonight. Now." He had another house in Boca Raton, but Walter had never seen it.

"I thought we were going to stay for the snow."

"I'm selling it. I've put it on the market."

"Look, I've got negatives drying. What am I supposed to do?" He tried to keep his voice level in contrast to Buck's which was skidding.

"Do whatever you want. But do it somewhere else. Go see Albina Muth."

"Look –"

"I'm sick and tired of having a tenant in my car. The Mercedes actually smells, it stinks, or haven't you noticed? The car is ruined. I'm sick and tired of listening to Albina Muth suck up my coffee. And I'm tired of you. In fact, you can have the car, the stinking car you ruined. Get in it and get out. Now."

"Look, this is ironic. Albina Muth is not coming back. She took all her stuff out of the car. This was it. Today. I took some pictures and that was it."

Buck B. looked toward the black window, toward the mountain drowned in the canyon of night, still seeing the slope stripped of trees, strewn with rammel and broken slash, and beyond this newly cleared slope another hill and the field with the poorhouse visible for the first time through the binoculars.

"Get out," he said through his nose, limping forward and raising Barb Cigar's ex-father-in-law's sabre. "Get out."

Walter almost laughed, old Buck B. with his red face and waving a Polish sabre. The Mercedes wasn't a bad consolation prize. He could have the interior steam-cleaned or deodorized or something. All he had to do was run back down the stairs, get the negatives and exit, this way out, one way to the Mercedes. He tried it.

Harold Edgerton. *Cutting the Card Quickly*, **1964. Dye transfer print.** (Courtesy Palm Press, Inc. Copyright © The Harold E. Edgerton 1992 Trust)

Shots

C Y N T H I A   O Z I C K

I came to photography as I came to infatuation – with no special talent for it, and with no point of view. Taking pictures – when *I* take
them, I mean – has nothing to do with art and less to do with reality.
I'm blind to what intelligent people call "composition," I revile every
emanation of "grain," and any drag through a gallery makes me want
to die. As for the camera as *machine* – well, I know the hole I have to
look through, and I know how to press down with my finger. The rest
is thingamajig. What brought me to my ingenious profession was no
idea of the Photograph as successor to the Painting, and no pleasure
in darkrooms, or in any accumulation of clanking detritus.

Call it necrophilia. I have fallen in love with corpses. Dead faces
draw me. I'm uninformed about the history of photography – 1832,
the daguerreotype, mercury vapor; what an annoyance that so blatant
a thing as picture-taking is considered worth applying a history to! –
except to understand how long a past the camera has, measured by a
century-old length of a woman's skirt. People talk of inventing a time
machine, as if it hadn't already been invented in the box and shutter.
I have been ravished by the last century's faces, now motes in their
graves – such lost eyes, and noses, and mouths, and earlobes, and
dress-collars: my own eyes soak these up; I can never leave off looking at anything brown and brittle and old and decaying at the edges.

The autumn I was eleven I found the Brown Girl. She was under a
mound of chestnut-littered leaves near five tall trash barrels in a cor-

ner of the yard behind the Home for the Elderly Female Ill. Though the old-lady inmates were kept confined to a high balcony above the browning grass of their bleak overgrown yard, occasionally I would see some witless half-bald refugee shuffling through a weed-sea with stockings rolled midway down a sinewy blue calf engraved by a knotted garter. They scared me to death, these sticks and twigs of brainless ancients, rattling their china teeth and howling at me in foreign tongues, rolling the bright gems of their mad old eyes inside their nearly visible crania. I used to imagine that if one of these fearful witches could just somehow get beyond the gate, she would spill off garters and fake teeth and rheumy eye-whites and bad smells and stupid matted old flesh, and begin to bloom all plump and glowing and ripe again: Shangri-La in reverse.

What gave me this imagining was the Brown Girl. Any one of these pitiful decaying sacks might once have been the Brown Girl. If only someone had shot a kind of halt-arrow through the young nipples of the Brown Girl at the crest of her years, if only she had been halted, arrested, stayed in her ripeness and savor!

The Brown Girl lived. She lay in a pile of albums dumped into the leaves. It seemed there were hundreds of her: a girl in a dress that dropped to the buttons of her shoes, with an arched bosom and a hint of bustle, and a face mysteriously shut: you never once saw her teeth, you never once saw the lips in anything like the hope of a smile; laughter was out of the question. A grave girl; a sepia girl; a girl as brown as the ground. She must have had her sorrows.

Gradually (to my eyes suddenly) I saw her age. It wasn't that the plain sad big-nosed face altered: no crinkles at the lids, no grooves digging out a distinct little parallelogram from nostril-sides to mouth-ends – or, if these were in sight, they weren't what I noticed. The face faded out – became not there. The woman turned to ghost. The ghost wore different clothes now, too familiar to gape at. The fingers were ringless. The eyes whitened off. Somehow for this melancholy spinster's sake the first rule of the box camera was always being violated: not to put the sun behind your subject. A vast blurred drowning orb of sun flooded massively, habitually down from the upper right corner of her picture. Whoever photographed her, over years and years and years, meant to obliterate her. But I knew it was no sun-bleach that conspired to efface her. What I was seeing – what I *had* seen – was time. And not time on the move, either, the illusion of stories and movies. What I had seen was time as stasis, time at the standstill, time at the fix; the time (though I hadn't yet reached it in school) of Keats's Grecian urn. The face faded out because death was coming: death the changer, the collapser, the witherer; death the bleacher, blancher, whitener.

The truth is, I'm looked on as a close-mouthed professional, serious about my trade, who intends to shut up and keep secrets when necessary. I repel all "technical" questions – if someone wants to discuss the make of my camera (it's Japanese), or my favorite lens, or some trick I might have in developing, or what grade of paper I like, I'll stare her down. Moonings on Minor White's theories I regard as absolutely demeaning. I have a grasp on what I am about, and it isn't any of that.

What it is, is the Brown Girl. I kept her. I kept her, I mean, in a pocket of my mind (and one of her pictures in the pocket of my blouse); I kept her because she was dead. What I expect you to take from this is that I *could* keep her *even though* she was dead. I wasn't infatuated by her (not that she was the wrong sex: infatuation, like any passion of recognition, neglects gender); she was too oppressed and brown and quiet for that. But it was she who gave me the miraculous hint: a hint derived from no science of mechanics or physics, a rapturous hint on the other side of art, beyond metaphor, deep in the wonderfully literal. What she made me see was that if she wasn't a girl anymore, if she wasn't a woman anymore, if she was very likely not even a member of the elderly female ill anymore (by the time her photos fell among the leaves, how long had she been lying under them?), still I *had* her, actually and physically and with the certainty of simple truth. I could keep her, just as she used to be, because someone had once looked through the bunghole of a box and clicked off a lever. Whoever had desultorily drowned her in too much sun had anyhow given her a monument two inches wide and three inches long. What happened then was here now. I had it in the pocket of my blouse.

Knowing this – that now will become then, that huge will turn little – doesn't cure. I walk around the wet streets with a historian now, a tenured professor of South American history: he doesn't like to go home to his wife. Somehow it always rains when we meet, and it's Sam's big blue umbrella, with a wooden horse's head for a handle, that preoccupies me this instant. Which is strange: he hasn't owned it for a whole year. It was left in a yellow garish coffee shop on the night side of a street you couldn't trust, and when Sam went back, only ten minutes later, to retrieve it, of course it wasn't there.

At that time I didn't care about one thing in Sam's mind. I had to follow him, on assignment, all through a course of some public symposia he was chairing. We had – temporarily – the same employer. His college was setting up a glossy little booklet for the State Department to win South American friends with: I had to shoot Sam on the podium with Uruguayans, Sam on the podium with Brazilians, Sam on the podium with Peruvians, and so forth. It was a lackluster job – I had just come, not so long ago, from photographing an intergalactic physicist whose bravest hope was the invention of an alphabet to shoot into the kindergartens of the cosmos – so it was no trouble at all not to listen to the speeches while I shot the principals. Half the speeches were in Portuguese or Spanish, and if you wanted to you could put on earphones anywhere in the hall and hear a simultaneous translation. The translator sat at the squat end of the long symposium table up on the stage with Sam and the others, but kept his microphone oddly close to his lips, like a kiss, sweat sliding and gleaming along his neck – it seemed he was tormented by that bifurcated concentration. His suffering attracted me. He didn't count as one of the principals – the celebrity of the day (now it was night, the last of the dark raining afternoon) was the vice-consul of Chile – but I shot him anyhow, for my own reasons: I liked the look of that shining sweat on his bulging Adam's apple. I calculated my aim (I'm very fast at this), shot once, shot again, and was amazed to see blood spring out of a hole in his neck. The audience fell apart – it was like watching an anthill after you've kicked into it; there was a spaghetti of wires and police; the simultaneous translator was dead. It made you listen for the simultaneous silence of the principal speaker, but the Chilean vice-consul only swerved his syllables into shrieks, with his coat over his head; he was walked away in a tremor between two colleagues suddenly sprouting guns. A mob of detectives took away my film; it was all I could do to keep them from arresting my camera. I went straight to Sam – it was his show – to complain. "That's *film* in there, not bullets." "It's evidence now," Sam said. "Who wanted to do that?" I said. "God knows," Sam said; "they didn't do what they wanted anyhow," and offered six political possibilities, each of which made it seem worthwhile for someone to do away with the Chilean vice-consul. He found his umbrella under the table and steered me out. The rain had a merciless wind in it, and every glassy sweep of it sent fountains spitting upward from the pavement. We stood for a while under his umbrella (he gripping the horse's head hard enough to whiten his knuckles) and watched them carry the simultaneous translator out. He was alone on a stretcher; his duality was done, his job as surrogate consummated. I reflected how quickly vertical becomes horizontal. "You knew him," I said.

"Only in a public way. He's been part of all these meetings."

"So have I," I said.

"I've watched you watching me."

I resisted this. "That's professional watching. It's more like stalking. I always stalk a bit before I shoot."

"You talk like a terrorist," Sam said, and began a history of South American conspiracy, which group was aligned with whom, who gave asylum, who withheld it, who the Chilean vice-consul's intimates across several borders were, at this instant plotting vengeance. He had exactly the kind of mentality – cumulative, analytical – I least admired, but since he also had the only umbrella in sight, I stuck with him. He was more interested in political factionalism – he had to get everything sorted out, and his fascination seemed to be with the victims – than in his having just sat two feet from a murder. "My God," I said finally, "doesn't the power of inaccuracy impress you? It could've been you on that stretcher."

"I don't suppose *you* ever miss your target," he said.

"No," I said, "but I don't shoot to kill."

"Then you're not one of those who want to change the world," he said, and I could smell in this the odor of his melancholy. He was a melancholic and an egotist; this made me a bit more attentive. His umbrella, it appeared, was going to pilot him around for miles and miles; I went along as passenger. We turned at last into a coffee shop – this wasn't the place he lost the horse's head in – and then turned out again, heated up, ready for more weather. "Don't you ever go home?" I asked him.

"Don't you?"

"I live alone."

"I don't. I hate my life," he said.

"I don't blame you. You've stuffed it up with South American facts."

"Would you like North American facts better?"

"I can't take life in whole continents," I protested.

"The thing about taking it in continents is that you don't have to take it face by face."

"The faces are the best part."

"Some are the worst," Sam said.

I looked into his; he seemed a victim of factionalism himself, as if you become what you study. He had rather ferocious eyes, much too shiny, like something boiling in a pot – the ferocity made you think them black, but really they were pale – and black ripe rippled hair and unblemished orderly teeth, not white but near-white. "Which faces are the worst?"

"Now I'll go home," he said.

The murder had cut short the series of symposia; the South Americans scattered, which was too bad – they were Sam's source of vitality. But it never occurred to either of us that we might not meet again officially, and often enough we did – he on a platform, myself with camera. Whether this meant that all the magazine people I knew – the ones who were commissioning my pictures – were all at once developing a fevered concern for South American affairs (more likely it was for terrorism) is a boring question. I know *I* wasn't. I never wanted to listen to Sam on the subjects he was expert in, and I never did. I only caught what I thought of as their "moans" – impure and simmering and winnowing and sad. The sounds that came through his microphone were always intensely public: he was, his audience maintained – loyalists, they trotted after him from speech to speech – a marvelous generalist. He could go from predicting the demand for bauxite to tracing migrations of Indian populations, all in a single stanza. He could connect disparate packets of contemporary information with a linking historic insight that took your breath away. He was a very, very good public lecturer; all his claque said so. He could manage to make anyone (or everyone but me) care about South America. Still, I had a little trick in my head as he declaimed and as I popped my flashbulbs, not always at him – more often at the

distinguished sponsors of the event. I could tell they were distinguished from the way they dragged me up to the dais to photograph
them – it showed how important they were. Sometimes they wanted
to be photographed just before Sam began, and sometimes, with
their arms around him, when he was just finished, themselves grinning into Sam's applause. All the while I kept the little trick going.

The little trick was this: whatever he said that was vast and public
and South American, I would simultaneously translate (I hoped I
wouldn't be gunned down for it) into everything private and personal
and secret. This required me to listen shrewdly to the moan behind
the words – I had to blot out the words for the sake of the tune.
Sometimes the tune would be civil or sweet or almost jolly – especially if he happened to get a look at me before he ascended to his
lectern – but mainly it would be narrow and drab and resigned. I
knew he had a wife, but I was already thirty-six, and who didn't have
a wife by then? I wasn't likely to run into them if they didn't.
Bachelors wouldn't be where I had to go, particularly not in public
halls gaping at the per capita income of the interior villages of the
Andes, or the future of Venezuelan oil, or the fortunes of the last
Paraguayan bean crop, or the differences between the centrist parties
in Bolivia and Colombia, or whatever it was that kept Sam ladling
away at his tedious stew. I drilled through all these sober-shelled
facts into their echoing gloomy melodies: and the sorrowful sounds I
unlocked from their casings – it was like breaking open a stone and
finding the music of the earth's wild core boiling inside – came down
to the wife, the wife, the wife. That was the tune Sam was moaning
all the while: wife wife wife. He didn't like her. He wasn't happy with
her. His whole life was wrong. He was a dead man. If I thought
I'd seen a dead man when they took that poor fellow out on that
stretcher, I was stupidly mistaken; *he* was ten times deader than that.
If the terrorist who couldn't shoot straight had shot *him* instead, he

couldn't be more riddled with gunshot than he was this minute –
he was smoking with his own death.

In the yellow garish coffee shop he went on about his wife – he
shouldn't be telling me all this, my God, what the hell did he think
he was doing; he was a fool; he was a cliché; he was out of a cartoon
or an awful play; he was an embarrassment to himself and to me. It
was either a trance or a seizure. And then he forgot his umbrella, and
ran back after it, and it was gone. It wouldn't have had, necessarily, to
be a desperate thief who stole his horse's head that night; it might
easily have been a nice middle-class person like ourselves. A nice
middle-class person especially would have hated to be out in such a
drenching without a shred of defense overhead – Sam charged on
into gales of cold rain, and made me charge onward too: for the first
time he had me by the hand. I wouldn't let him keep it, though – I
had to bundle my camera under my coat.

"How long are we going to walk in this?" I said.

"We'll walk and walk."

"I've got to go home or I'll soak my equipment," I complained.

"I'm not going home."

"Don't you ever go home?"

"My whole life is wrong," he said.

We spilled ourselves into another coffee place and sat there till
closing. My shoes were seeping and seeping. He explained Verity: "I
admire her," he said. "I esteem her, you wouldn't believe how I esteem
that woman. She's a beautiful mother. She's strong and she's bright
and she's independent and there's nothing she can't do."

"Now tell her good points," I said.

"She can fix a car. She always fixes the car. Puts her head into
the hood and fixes it. She builds furniture. We live in a madhouse of
excess property – she built every stick of it. She saws like a madwoman. She *sews* like a madwoman – I don't mean just *clothes*. She

sews her own clothes and the girls' clothes too. What I mean is she *sews* – bedspreads and curtains and upholstery, even *car* upholstery. And she's got a whole budding career of her own. I've made her sound like a bull, but she's really very delicate at whatever she does – she does plates, you know."

"License plates?"

"She's done *some* metalwork – her minor was metallurgy – but what I'm talking about is ceramics. Porcelain. She does painted platters and pots and pitchers and sells them to Bloomingdale's."

"She's terrific," I said.

"She's terrific," he agreed. "There's nothing she can't do."

"Cook?"

"My God, *cook*," he said. "French, Italian, Indian, whatever you want. And bakes. Pastries, the difficult stuff, crusts made of cloud. She's a domestic genius. We have this big harp – hell, it was busted, a skeleton in a junk shop, so she bought it cheap and repaired it – she plays it like an angel. You think you're in heaven inside that hell. She plays the piano, too – classics, ragtime, rock. She's got a pretty nice singing voice. She's good at basketball – she practically never misses a shot. Don't ask me again if I admire her."

I asked him again if he admired her.

"I'm on my knees," he groaned. "She's a goddamn goddess. She's powerful and autonomous and a goddamn genius. Christ," he said, "I hate my life."

"If I had someone like that at home," I said, "I'd never be out in the rain."

"She could abolish the weather if she wanted to, only she doesn't want to. She has a terrific will."

I thought this over and was surprised by my sincerity: "You ought to go home," I told him.

"Let's walk."

After that we met more or less on purpose. The South American fad wore off – there was a let-up in guerrilla activity down there – and it got harder to find him in public halls, so I went up to his college now and then and sat in on his classes, and afterward, rain or shine, but mostly rain, we walked. He told me about his daughters – one of them was nearly as terrific as Verity herself – and we walked with our arms hooked. "Is something happening here?" I inquired. "Nothing will ever happen here," he said. We had a friend in common, the editor who'd assigned me to photographing that intergalactic physicist I've mentioned; it turned out we were asked, Sam with Verity, myself as usual, to the editor's party, in honor of the editor's ascension. There were some things the editor hadn't done which added immensely to his glory; and because of all the things he hadn't done they were making him vice-chancellor of Sam's college. I did justice to those illustrious gaps and omissions: I took the host, now majestic, and his wife, their children, their gerbil, their maid. I shot them embedded in their guests. I dropped all those pictures behind me like autumn leaves. I hadn't brought my usual Japanese spy, you see; I'd carried along a tacky Polaroid instead – instant development, a detective story without a detective, ah, I disliked that idea, but the evening needed its jester. I aimed and shot, aimed and shot, handing out portraits deciduously. Verity had her eye on all this promiscuity; she was blond and capacious and maybe capricious; she seemed without harm and without mercy.

"You're the one who shot the simultaneous translator," she said.

"Judicial evidence," I replied.

"Now let me," she said, "ask you something about your trade. In photography, do you consistently get what you expect?"

I said: "It's the same as life."

Verity expressed herself: "The viewfinder, the viewfinder!"

"I always look through that first," I admitted.

"And then do you get what you see? I mean can you predict exactly, or are you always surprised by what comes out?"

"I can never predict," I told her, "but I'm never surprised."

"That's fatalism," Verity said. Her voice was an iron arrow; she put her forefinger into my cheek as humbly as a bride. "Talk about shots, here's a parting one. You take a shot at Sam, no expectations. He's not like life. He's safe. He's *good*."

He was safe and he was good: Sam the man of virtue. She knew everything exactly, even when everything was nothing she knew it exactly, she was without any fear at all; jealousy wasn't in her picture; she was more virtuous than he was, she was big, she had her great engine, she was her own cargo. And you see what it is with infatuation: it comes on you as quick as a knife. It's a bullet in the neck. It gets you from the outside. One moment you're in your prime of health, the next you're in anguish. Until then – until I had the chance to see for myself how clear and proud his wife was – Sam was an entertainment, not so entertaining after all. Verity was the Cupid of the thing, Verity's confidence the iron arrow that dragged me down. She had her big foot on her sour catch. I saw in her glow, in her sureness, in her pride, in her tall ship's prow of certitude, the plausibility of everything she knew: he'd have to go home in the end.

But the end's always at the end; in the meantime there's the meantime.

How to give over these middle parts? I couldn't see what I looked like, from then on, to Sam: all the same I had my automatic intelligence – light acting on a treated film. I was treated enough; Verity had daubed me. Since I was soaked in her solution, infatuation took, with me, a mechanical form – if you didn't know how mechanical it was, you would have imagined it was sly. I could listen now to everything Sam said. Without warning, I could *follow* him; I discovered myself in the act of wanting more. I woke up one morning in a fit of curiosity about the quantity of anthracite exports on the Brazilian littoral. I rooted in hard-to-find volumes of Bolívar's addresses. I penetrated the duskier hells of the public library and boned up on every banana republic within reach. It was astounding: all at once, and for no reason – I mean for *the* reason – Sam interested me. It was like walking on the lining of his brain.

On the South American issue he was dense as a statue. He had never noticed that I hadn't paid attention to his subject before; he didn't notice that I was attentive now. His premise was that everyone alive without exception was all the time infatuated with the former Spanish Empire. On *my* subject, though, Sam was trying; it was because of Verity; she had made him ambitious to improve himself with me.

"Verity saw at that party," he said, "that you had the kind of camera that gets you the picture right away."

"Not exactly right away. You have to wait a minute," I corrected.

"Why don't you use a camera like that all the time? It's magic. It's like a miracle."

"Practical reasons of the trade. The farther you are from having what you think you want, the more likely you are to get it. It's just that you have to wait. You really have to *wait*. What's important is the waiting."

Sam didn't get it. "But it's *chemistry*. The image is already on the film. It's the same image one minute later or two months later."

"You're too miracle-minded even for a historian," I admonished him. "It's not like that at all. If you have a change of heart between shooting your picture and taking it out of the developer, the picture changes too." I wanted to explain to him how, between the exposure and the solution, history comes into being, but telling that would make me bleed, like a bullet in the neck, so I said instead, "Photography is *literal*. It gets what's *there*."

Meanwhile the rain is raining on Sam and me. We meet in daylight now, and invent our own occasions. We hold hands, we hook arms, we walk through the park. There is a mole on his knuckle which has attached itself to my breathing; my lungs grasp all the air they can. I want to lay my tears on the hairs of his fingers. Because of the rain, the daylight is more like twilight; in this perpetual half of dusk, the sidewalks a kind of blackened purple, like fallen plums, we talk about the past and the future of the South American continent. Verity is in her house. I leave my camera behind too. Our faces are rivers, we walk without an umbrella, the leaves splash. When I can't find Sam on my own, I telephone Verity; she stops the motor of her sewing machine and promises to give him the message when he returns. He comes flying out to meet me, straight from his Committee on Inter-American Conditions; I'm practically a colleague now, and a pleasure to talk to about Ecuadorian peonage. He tells me he's never had a mistress and never will; his wife is too remarkable. I ask him whether he's ever walked in a summer rain this way with anyone else. He admits he has; he admits it hasn't lasted. "The rain hasn't lasted? Or the feeling?" He forgets to answer. I remember that *he* is only interested; it's I who feel. We talk some more about the native religions still hiding out in the pampas; we talk about the Jewish gauchos in nineteenth-century Argentina. He takes it all for granted. He doesn't realize how hard I've had to study. A big leaf like a pitcher overturns itself all over our heads, and we make a joke about Ponce de Léon and the Fountain of Youth. I ask him then if he'll let me take his picture in the park, under a dripping linden tree, in a dangerous path, so that I can keep him forever, in case it doesn't last.

I see that he doesn't understand. He doesn't understand: unlike me, he's not under any special spell, he's not in thrall to any cult. That's the rub always – infatuation's unilateral or it doesn't count as real. I think he loves me – he may even be "in love"– but he's not caught like me. He'd never trace my life over as I've traced over his brain waves. He asks me why I want to shoot him under the linden tree. I tell him the truth I took from his wife: virtue ravishes me. I want to keep its portrait. I am silent about the orphaned moment we're living in now, how it will leave us. I feel, I feel our pathos. We are virtue's orphans. The tree's green shoots are fleeting; all green corrupts to brown. Sam denies that he's a man of virtue. It's only his guilt about Verity: she's too terrific to betray.

He consents to having his picture taken in the sopping park if I agree to go home with him afterward.

I say in my amazement, "I can't go home with you. She's *there*."

"She's always there."

"Then how can I go home with you?"

"You have to *see*. It's all been too obscure. I want you to know what I know."

"I know it, you've told me. You've told and told."

"You have to get the smell of it. Where I am and how I live. Otherwise you won't believe in it. You won't know it," he insists. "Such cozy endurances."

"You endure them," I said.

"Yesterday," he said, "she brought home a box of old clothes from the Salvation Army. From a thrift shop. From an old people's home, who knows where she got it from. Pile of rags. She's going to sew them into God's bright ribbons. A patchwork quilt. She'll spin straw into gold, you'll see."

"She's terrific."

"She's a terrific wife," he says.

We walk to my place, pick up my camera – I stop to grab my light meter for the rain's sake – and walk crosstown to the park again. I shoot Sam, the man of virtue, under the dripping linden tree. Although I am using my regular equipment, it seems to me the picture's finished on the spot. It's as if I roll it out and fix it then and there. Sam has got his back against the bark, and all the little wet leaves lick down over his bumpy hair. He resembles a Greek runner resting. His face is dappled by all those heart-shaped leaves, and I know that all the rest of my life I'll regret not having shot him in the open, in a field. But my wish for now is to speckle him and see him darkle under the rainy shade of a tree. It comes to me that my desire – oh, my desire! it stings me in the neck – is just now not even for Sam's face: it's for the transitoriness of these thin vulnerable leaves, with their piteous veins turned upward toward a faintness of liverish light.

We walk the thirty-one blocks, in the quickening rain, to his place. It's only a four-room apartment, but Verity's made a palace of it. Everything plain is converted into a sweetness, a furriness, a thickness of excess. She weaves, she knits. She's an immense spider building out of her craw. The floors are piled with rugs she's woven, the chairs with throws she's knit. She's cemented up a handy little fireplace without a flue; it really works, and on a principle she invented herself. She's carpentered all the bookcases – I catch the titles of the four books Sam's written; he's a dignitary and a scholar, after all – and overhead there wafts and dazzles the royal chandelier she found in the gutter and refurbished. Each prism slid through her polishing and perfecting fingers. Verity resurrects, Verity's terrific – you can't avoid thinking it. She's got her big shoulders mounted over her sewing machine in the corner of the living room, hemming brown squares. "It's weird, you wouldn't believe it," she says, "*all* the stuff in this box they gave me is brown. It's good rich fabric, though – a whole load of clothes from dead nuns. You know what happened? A convent dissolved, the young nuns broke their vows and ran to get married."

"That's *your* story," Sam says.

Verity calls her daughter – only one of the girls is at home, the other is away at college. Clearly this one isn't the daughter that's so much like Verity. She has a solemn hard flank of cheek, and no conversation. She carries out a plate of sliced honey cake and three cups of tea; then she hides herself in her bedroom. A radio is in there;

gilded waves of Bach tremble out of it. I look around for Verity's harp.

"Hey, let's dress you up," Verity says out of her teacup; she's already downed a quantity of cake. "There's stuff in that box that would just fit you. You've got a waist like our girls. I wish I had a waist like that." I protest; I tell her it's too silly. Sam smolders with his sour satisfaction, and she chums her palms inside the box like a pair of oars. She pulls out a long skirt, and a blouse called a bodice, and another blouse to wear under that, with long sleeves. Sam pokes my spine and nudges me into the girl's bedroom, where there's a tall mirror screwed into the back of the door. I look at myself.

"Period piece," says Verity.

I'm all in brown, as brown as leaves. The huge high harp, not gold as I imagined it but ivory, is along the wall behind me. I believe everything Sam has told about the conquistadores. I believe everything he's told about Verity. He's a camera who never lies. His wet hair is black as olives. He belongs to his wife, who's terrific. She's put a nun's bonnet on herself. She has an old-fashioned sense of fun – the words come to me out of, I think, Louisa May Alcott: she likes costume and dress-up. Soon she will have us guessing riddles and playing charades. They are a virtuous and wholesome family. The daughter, though her look is bone, is fond of Bach; no junk music in such a household. They are sweeter than the whole world outside. When Sam is absent the mother and her daughter climb like kittens into a knitted muff.

I shoot Verity wearing the nun's bonnet.

"Look at *you*!" she cries.

I return to the mirror to see. I am grave; I have no smile. My face is mysteriously shut. I'm suffering. Lovesick and dreamsick, I'm dreaming of my desire. I am already thirty-six years old, tomorrow I will be forty-eight years old, and a crafty parallelogram begins to frame the space between my nose and mouth. My features are very distinct – I will live for years and years before they slide out of the mirror. I'm the Brown Girl in the pocket of my blouse. I reek of history. If, this minute, I could glide into a chemical solution, as if in a gondola, splashed all over and streaming with wet silver, would the mirror seize and fix me, like a photographic plate? I watch Sam's eyes, poached and pale and mottled with furious old civilizations, steaming hatred for his wife. I trip over the long drapery of my nun's hem. All the same I catch up my camera without dropping it – my ambassador of desire, my secret house with its single shutter, my chaste aperture, my dead infant, husband of my bosom. Their two heads, hers light, his black, negatives of each other, are caught side by side in their daughter's mirror. I shoot into their heads, the white harp behind. Now they are exposed. Now they will stick forever.

The Swollen Face

ALBERTO MORAVIA

For a long stretch of the Via Appia they walked in silence along the grassy verge, passing the gates of villas one after another, the cypresses and pines at the roadside appearing discolored and dust-covered against a scirocco-darkened sky. The grass, burnt up by the sultry weather, seemed to crumble beneath their feet; waste paper, tins, newspapers left behind by picnickers covered the ground wherever there was the agreeable shade of a big tree or the picturesque presence of a ruin. It was the hottest and most deserted time of day; only a few cars went past, bumping over the big stones of the Roman pavement. Livio, looking sideways at his wife, said suddenly: "What's the matter with you? Your face is swollen as though you had toothache."

It was true: his wife's round, pretty face had a congested, inflated look; and this not only in its shape but also in its unhealthily flushed, dense color. "There's nothing wrong with me," she said, her teeth clenched; "what's come into your head?"

But by now they had reached the rustic gate of the villa in which the film star lived. The low wall was covered by climbing rosebushes with little yellow flowers. "Here we are," said Livio, and turned off into a field, along the boundary wall. It was a piece of waste ground, with scattered garbage piles that must have been still fresh, for they threw out, in the heat, a strong, acid smell. Far away, beyond the edge of a precipitous slope, could be seen a pale line of distant concrete buildings, with a livid light upon them beneath the dark sky. Livio followed the wall to a point where it turned at right angles, then stopped, put aside the branches of the rosebushes so as to make an opening for the lens of his camera, adjusted the sights and then said: "From here you can see the open space in front of the house. She's bound to come out. Of course she'll come out."

"Supposing she doesn't?"

"She's bound to."

From one of the trash piles Livio took an old gas can, turned it upside down and sat on it, his camera on his knees, his face at the opening, between two bars of the railing. His wife, behind him, asked: "How many times have you been here already?"

"This is the fifth time."

"You're determined, aren't you, to get this photograph?"

Livio noticed something malicious and provoking in his wife's question, but he attached no importance to it and, without taking his face away from the opening, answered: "I'm determined because it will sell very well."

"Or for some other reason?"

Beyond the garden and the graveled open space, Livio could see the façade of the red-painted villa, the row of vases planted with lemon trees along the terrace, the door framed in white marble under a tiled porch. Slightly to the right of the door could be glimpsed the front part of an enormous American car, black and with dazzling chromium plate, very like a hearse. In the dull scirocco light the fine gravel of the drive seemed to be pulsating with a swarming life of its own which made one feel dizzy. Livio turned his face from the opening and inquired with sudden irritation: "*What* other reason?"

His wife was now wandering about around the pile of trash on which he was seated, in a state of feverish, menacing agitation like that of a wild beast in a cage. She suddenly whisked around. "D'you really think I don't understand?"

"But *what?*"

"That you want to get this photograph of her so as to have an excuse for approaching her and visiting her and then, by degrees, becoming her lover."

In his astonishment Livio, for a moment, found nothing to say. Finally he pronounced slowly: "Is that what you think?"

"Certainly," she said, in an irresolute yet stubborn tone of voice, as though she too were aware of the absurdity of the accusation but had nevertheless privately made up her mind to maintain it at all costs.

"D'you really think that I, Livio Millefiorini, a shabby, down-at-heel photographer, would aspire to become the lover of a film star who is famous all over the world, who is a multimillionairess, and who, into the bargain, is well provided with a husband, not to mention a number of suitors?"

His wife's round, childish face, more swollen-looking than ever, expressed at the same time both indecision and obstinacy. At length she said impudently: "Well, yes, that's what I think." She took a kick at an empty can and went on: "D'you think I didn't notice your disappointment today when I said I wanted to come with you? And your delight, on those other days, when I said I *wouldn't* come with you?"

"But, Lucia . . ."

"You want to have an excuse for getting into touch with her. You'll take a photograph and then you'll telephone her and so you'll meet and make love."

Livio looked at her; then with sudden haste he put his eye to the opening: he thought he had caught sight of something moving on the open space. It was not the film star, however, but two large poodles, of a dirty white not very different from the color of the gravel. They rolled about, nibbling at each other, and then rushed off around the corner of the villa and vanished. Livio turned around again and said with profound conviction: "You're mad. Now I understand why you have a swollen face today. You're swollen with jealousy."

"No, I'm not mad. And I'll take this opportunity of telling you: I'm fed up, fed up, fed up."

Livio wondered whether it would not be a good plan, while he was waiting for the invisible film star, to take some interesting photograph in the meantime. He suddenly noticed something glittering, on the top step in front of the door. He put his eyes to the lens and saw that it was two glasses and a bottle of whiskey. Perhaps, he thought, the star and her husband had sat on the step, possibly the evening before, to have a little tipple and look at the full moon as it appeared behind the cypresses of the Via Appia. "A glass of whiskey in the moonlight, sitting unceremoniously on the doorstep: that's the title," thought Livio as he took the photograph and at once reloaded his camera. Behind him, he heard his wife repeat: "Yes, I'm utterly fed up."

"Fed up with what?"

"With everything, and in the first place with you. If you even loved me . . . But you don't love me; it's barely two years since we were married and you're running after all the women.

"But when, when . . . ?"

"You run after all the women, and therefore certain things which I might have put up with if you loved me have become unendurable."

"But what things?"

"What things? Well listen, I'll tell you them all. The furnished room with the window on the courtyard, with no separate entrance and with the 'use' of a kitchen. Buses and trams. Meals standing up in a snack bar. Third-rate cinemas. Television at the dairy. And look here – look!"

Livio looked; there was something compelling in the tone of the exasperated voice. Standing on a pile of trash, his wife had pulled up her skirt a little and was showing him the patched edge of her undergarment and the long darns in the stockings on her thin legs. "Look!" she said; "my underclothes are in tatters, I wear stockings like spiders' webs, and shoes down at the heels, and this dress is two years old. And the baby is wrapped in rags and has a drawer for his cradle. Isn't that enough for you?"

Livio frowned and tried to reason with her. "I started only a short time ago. I had to spend all my money on fitting up a studio. Now I shall start to have some income."

But by this time his wife was no longer listening to him. "Besides," she said, "I must also tell you, I don't like your profession."

Livio once again put his face to the opening among the rosebushes. The glass door under the tiled porch had now opened and a manservant in a white jacket appeared. The man stopped, took the whiskey bottle and the two glasses and vanished. Livio took a photograph of this also, reloaded his camera and then turned round and said, with intense irritation: "So you don't like my profession? Why ever not? It's just as good as any other, isn't it?"

"No," she cried angrily, "it's not just as good as any other. It's a despicable profession. You spend your time annoying people who have done you no harm and whose only fault is that they are well known. You persecute them, you're ruthless with them, you won't leave them in peace. You're incapable of love yourself and you spy on the love of those who do love, you have no real life of your own and you try to portray the lives of those who do have real lives, you're a penniless wretch yourself and you photograph the luxury and the amusements of those who have money. And I tell you, too, that when certain things happen – like the thing that happened the other evening at the door of that nightclub, when that actor started kicking you – then I'm ashamed of you. Because, instead of standing up to him, all you tried to do was to get as many photographs of him as you could, and I really believe that, if you'd been able to, you'd have actually photographed his foot at the moment when it was kicking your behind, and then you'd have been happy." She laughed, came down off the trash pile and stopped at a short distance from him. Livio took a quick glance through the opening, saw that the space in front of the house was still deserted, then turned around and cried: "You'll be sorry for these things that you're saying to me."

"The hour of truth has arrived," she said with some solemnity; "I'm fed up, fed up. Fed up with your photographs that nobody buys, fed up with hearing you talk about your contemptible exploits, fed up with hoping for better days. You would photograph anything in the world if it could be useful to you, even our own private life. In fact you've already done so."

"What d'you mean?"

"Yes, you've done it, you took a photograph of me at the beach, in a bikini, standing in front of a hut, and the picture was published with the title 'Rainy May. But some people are already thinking of swimming.'"

Livio shrugged. "But you were perfectly willing to be taken."

"Yes, and I caught a cold."

"But will you please tell me what you want of me?"

He saw her look disconcerted for a moment; then she said: "I want you to give up lying in wait in this stupid way, and then we can go."

"Are you still convinced that I want to become the film star's lover?"

"Yes."

"Well, I'm not going to give in to you. I've decided to get this photograph, and get it I shall."

His attention had been distracted while he was speaking. But now he turned and saw, through the tangle of rosebushes, that there was something going on, over on the space in front of the house: in fact the star herself opened the glass door under the tiled porch and appeared in the doorway. Livio recognized the straw-colored hair, the plump, thickly powdered face, the large, heavily made-up eyes, the big red mouth, the celebrated enormous bosom which peeped out above her bodice in two closely-pressed swellings. She lifted her bag up to the level of her bosom, fumbled in it, drew out a pair of dark glasses and put them on. Then she raised her arm and gave a shout. At once a dark shadow rushed across the lens: it was her chauffeur. She looked down, then walked over toward the car. She was dressed in a ridiculous way, like a doll, in a tight, pale-blue bodice and a wide, flower-patterned crinoline skirt which revealed legs of a chalky whiteness.

Now or never, thought Livio. He lifted the camera and started following her with it as she walked across the open space, ready to take the photograph at the moment when she was getting into the car. But all of a sudden he felt some shapeless, massive object come crashing down on him, causing him to fall off the gas can on which he was standing. When he got up, he saw his wife running away over the field toward the Via Appia, clutching his camera in her hand.

For a short while he stood still, angry and disappointed, his eyes filled with tears. Then, resigned, he walked away slowly toward the road. But he was brought to a halt: the star's long black car was passing, at that moment, right in front of him; here was another photograph that his wife had prevented him from taking. The car went off into the distance; he looked up and saw his wife coming toward him, holding the camera. Her face was no longer either swollen or red; she had given vent to her feelings; and she was smiling at him. As she came up to him she said: "Now you can take a photograph of *me*. It's a very long time since you promised to, but you can never make up your mind."

Bill Brandt. *Graham Greene*, 1948.
Gelatin silver print.
(Copyright © 1948 Bill Brandt)

Greene

PAUL THEROUX

The Ritz bar was empty, quiet, but crazed with decoration. I tried to get a fix on it. It was white, with a Bischof gleam, gold-trimmed mirrors that repeated its Edwardian flourishes of filigree and cigar wrappers, frosty statuettes, velvet, and the illusion of crystal in etched glass. The chocolate box of a whore's boudoir. I guessed I would have to lie on my belly to get the shot I wanted, but then I noticed in all that tedious gilt a man behind the bar polishing a goblet. He wore a white dinner jacket and was bald; his head shone. I saw at once how the crown of his skull gathered the whole room and miniaturized it, and he wore it like a map pasted to his dome. Shoot him nodding and you've got a vintage Weegee.

"A very good evening to you, madam."

I thought: You're kidding! I said, "A large gin and tonic."

"Kew," he said, and handed it over.

"You're welcome," I said. I expected him to take a swing at me, but he only picked up another goblet and continued his polishing. What a head! It made the wide-angle lens obsolete. But I didn't have the heart to do him. In fact, since arriving in London I had begun to feel winded and wheezy, a shortness of breath and a sort of tingling in my fingers and toes I put down to heartburn and jet lag.

Greene entered the bar at six sharp, a tall man in a dark blue suit, slightly crumpled, with an impressive head and a rather large brooding jaw. I almost fainted: it was my brother Orlando, a dead ringer.

Ollie had grown old in my mind like this. Greene's face, made hand-some by fatigue, had a sagging summer redness. He could have passed for a clergyman – he had that same assured carriage, the bored pitying lips, the gentle look of someone who has just stopped pray-ing. And yet there was about his look of piety an aspect of raffishness; about his distinguished bearing an air of anonymity; and whether it was caution or breeding, a slight unease in his hands. Like someone out of uniform, I thought, a general without his medals, a bishop who's left his robes upstairs, a happy man not quite succeeding at a scowling disguise. His hair was white, suggesting baldness at a dis-tance, and while none of his features was remarkable, together they created an extraordinary effect of unshakable dignity, the courtly ferocity you see in very old lions.

And something else, the metaphysical doohickey fame had printed lightly on his face – a mastery of form. One look told me he had no boss, no rivals, no enemies, no deadlines, no hates: not a grumbler, not a taker of orders. He was free: murder to photograph.

He said, "Miss Pratt?"

A neutral accent, hardly English, with a slight gargle, a glottal stop that turned my name into *Pgatt*.

"Mister Greene," I said.

"So glad you could make it."

We went to a corner table and talked inconsequentially, and it was there, while I was yattering, that I noticed his eyes. They were pale blue and depthless, with a curious icy light that made me think of a creature who can see in the dark – the more so because they were also the intimidating eyes of a blind man, with a hypnotist's unblinking blue. His magic was in his eyes, but coldly blazing they gave away nothing but this warning of indestructible certainty. When he stared at me I felt as if it were no use confessing – he knew my secrets. This inspired in me a sense of overwhelming hopelessness. Nothing I could tell him would be of the slightest interest to him: he'd heard it before, he'd been there, he'd done it, he'd known. I was extremely frightened: I had never expected to see Orlando again or to feel so naked.

I said, "How did you happen to get my name?"

"I knew it," said Greene. Of course. Then he added, "I've followed your work with enormous interest."

"The feeling's mutual."

"I particularly like your portrait of Evelyn Waugh."

"That's a story," I said. "I was in London. Joe Ackerley said Waugh was at the Dorchester, so I wrote him a note saying how much I enjoyed his books and that I wanted to do him. A reply comes, but it's not addressed to me. It's to *Mister* Pratt and it says something like, 'We have laws in this country restraining women from writing importuning letters to strange men. You should have a word with your wife' – that kind of thing. Pretty funny all the same."

Greene nodded. "I imagine your husband was rather annoyed."

"There was no Mister Pratt," I said. "There still isn't."

Greene looked at me closely, perhaps wondering if I was going to bare my soul.

I said, "But I kept after Waugh and later on he agreed. He liked the picture, too, asked for more prints. It made him look baronial, lord of the manor – it's full of sunshine and cigar smoke. And, God, that suit! I think it was made out of a horse blanket."

"One of the best writers we've ever had," said Greene. "I saw him from time to time, mostly in the Fifties." He thought a moment, and moved his glass of sherry to his lips but didn't drink. "I was in and out of Vietnam then. You've been there, of course. I found your pictures of those refugees very moving."

"The refugees were me," I said. "Just more raggedy, that's all. I couldn't find the pictures I wanted, so I went up to Hué, but they gave me a lot of flak and wouldn't let me leave town. The military started leaning on me. They didn't care about winning the war – they wanted to keep it going. I felt like a refugee myself, with my bum hanging out and getting kicked around. That's why the pictures were good. I could identify with those people. Oh, I know what they say – 'How can she do it to those poor so-and-so's!' But, really, they were all versions of me. Unfortunately."

"Did you have a pipe?"

"Pardon?"

"Opium," said Greene.

"Lord no."

"They ought to legalize it for people our age," he said. "Once, in Hanoi, I was in an opium place. They didn't know me. They put me in a corner and made a few pipes for me, and just as I was dropping off to sleep I looked up and saw a shelf with several of my books on it. French translations. When I woke up I was alone. I took them down and signed them."

"Then what did you do?"

"I put them back on the shelf and went away. No one saw me, and I never went back. It's a very pleasant memory."

"A photographer doesn't have those satisfactions."

"What about your picture of Che Guevara?"

"Oh, that," I said. "I've seen it so many times I've forgotten I took it. I never get a byline on it. It's become part of the folklore."

"Some of us remember."

It is this photograph of Che that was on the posters, with the Prince Valiant hair and the beret, his face upturned like a saint on an ikon. I regretted it almost as soon as I saw it swimming into focus under the enlarger. It flattered him and simplified his face into an expression of suffering idealism. I had made him seem better than he was. It was the beginning of his myth, a deception people took for truth because it was a photograph. But I knew how photography lied and mistook light for fact. I got Che on a good day. Luck, nothing more.

"Pagan saints," I said. "That's what I used to specialize in. They seemed right for the age, the best kind of hero, the embattled loser. The angel with the human smell, the innocent, the do-gooder, the outsider, the perfect stranger. I was a great underdogger. They saw things no one else did, or at least I thought so then."

Greene said, "Only the outsider sees. You have to be a stranger to write about any situation."

"Debs," I said.

"Debs?" He frowned. "I didn't think that was your line at all."

"Eugene V. Debs, the reformer," I said. "I did him."

"That's right," said Greene, but he had begun to smile.

"Ernesto wasn't a grumbler," I said. "That's what I liked about him. Raúl was something else."

"When were you in Cuba?"

"Was it 'fifty-nine? I forget. I know it was August. I had wanted to go ever since Walker Evans took his sleazy pictures of those rotting houses. I mentioned this in an interview and the next thing I know I'm awarded the José Martí Scholarship to study God-knows-what at Havana U. Naturally I turned it down."

"But you went."

"With bells on. I had a grand time. I did Ernesto and I don't know how many tractors, and the Joe Palooka of American literature, Mister Hemingway."

"I met Fidel," said Greene. There was just a hint of boasting in it.

I said, "I owe him a letter."

"Interesting chap."

"I did him, too, but he wasn't terribly pleased with it. He wanted me to do him with his arms outstretched, like Christ of the Andes, puffing a two-dollar cigar. No thank you. The one I did of him at Harvard is the best of the bunch – the hairy messiah bellowing at all those fresh-faced kids. Available light, lots of Old Testament drama."

Greene started to laugh. He had a splendid shoulder-shaking laugh, very infectious. It made his face redder, and he touched the back of his hand to his lips when he did it, like a small boy sneaking a giggle. Then he signaled to the waiter and said, "The same again."

"Isn't that Cuban jungle something?" I said.

"Yes, I liked traveling in Cuba," he said. "It could be rough, but not as rough as Africa." He put his hand to his lips again and laughed. "Do you know Jacqueline Bisset?"

"I don't think I've done her, no."

"An actress, very pretty. François Truffaut brought her down to Antibes last year. I gave them dinner and afterwards I began talking about Africa. She was interested that I'd been all over Liberia. 'But you stayed in good hotels?' she said. I explained that there weren't any hotels in the Liberian jungle. 'But you found restaurants?' she said. 'No,' I said, 'no restaurants at all.' This threw her a bit, but then she pressed me quite hard on everything else – the drinking water, the people, the weather, the wild animals and what-not. Finally, she asked me about my car. I told her I didn't have a car. A bus, maybe? No, I said, no bus. She looked at me, then said, 'Ah, I see how you are traveling – auto-stop!'"

"Pardon?"

"Hitchhiking."

"Bumming rides?"

"That's it – she thought I was hitchhiking through the Liberian jungle in 1935!" He laughed again. "I had to tell her there weren't any roads. She was astonished."

"Say no more. I know the type."

"But very pretty. You ought really to do her sometime."

"I did a series of pretty faces," I said. "My idea was to go to out-of-the-way places and get shots of raving beauties, who didn't know they were pretty. I did hundreds – farm girls, cashiers, housewives, girls lugging firewood, scullions, schoolgirls. A girl at a gas station, another one at a cosmetics counter in Filene's Basement."

"One sees them in the most unlikely places."

"These were heartbreaking. Afterwards, everyone said I'd posed them. But that was just it – the girls didn't have the slightest idea of why I was taking their pictures. Most of them were too poor to own mirrors. One was a knockout – a Spanish girl squatting with her skirt hiked up to her waist, sort of pouting, her bare bottom near her ankles. What a peach – there was a beautiful line cupping her bum and curving up her thigh to her knee. She didn't see me. And another one, a Chinese girl in Hong Kong I did after that Vietnam jaunt – long black hair, skin like porcelain, one of these willowy oriental bodies. She was plucking a chicken in a back alley in Kowloon, a tragic beauty with that half-starved holiness that fashion models make a mockery of. I weep when I think of it. That's partly because" – I leaned forward and whispered – "I've never told anyone this before – she was blind."

"You've done other blind people," said Greene. "I've seen them exhibited."

"When I was very young," I said slowly, trying to evade what was a fact. "I'm ashamed of it now. But the faces of the blind are never false – they are utterly naked. It was the only way I could practice my close-ups. They had no idea of what I was doing – that was the worst of it. But they had this amazing light, the whole face illuminated in beautiful repose. They're such strange pictures. I can't bear to look at them these days. I was blind myself. However, let's not go into that."

But as I described the pictures to Greene I saw that he had this same look on his own face, a blind man's luminous stare and that scarifying scrutiny in his features, his head cocked slightly to one side like a sightless witness listening for mistakes.

"I understand," he said.

"I'll be glad to show you the others," I said. "The pretty faces. You'll cry your eyes out."

"There were some lovely girls in Haiti," he said. "Many were prostitutes. Oh, I remember one night. I was with that couple I called the Smiths in my book. I said they were vegetarians. They weren't, but they were Americans. He was a fairly good artist. He could sketch pictures on the spot. We were at that bar I described in my book – the brothel. He picked one out and drew her picture, a terribly good likeness. All the girls came over to admire it." Greene paused to sip at his sherry, then he said, "She was a very attractive girl. If the Smiths hadn't been there I would have dated her myself."

It seemed a rather old-fashioned way of putting it – "dating" a hooker; but there was a lot of respectful admiration in his tone, none of the contempt one usually associates with the whore-hopper.

"Dated her," I said. "You mean a little boom-boom?"

"Jig-jig," he said. "But it comes to the same thing."

I laughed and said, "I really must be going."

"Have another drink," said Greene.

"Next time," I said. I had lost count of my gins, but I knew that as soon as I remembered how many I'd had I'd be drunk.

"Will you join me for dinner? I thought I might go across the street to Bentley's. That is, if you like fish."

I was tired, my bones ached, I felt woozy and I knew I was half pickled. I attributed all of this to my sudden transfer from Grand Island to London. But I also had a creeping sense of inertia, the slow alarm of sickness turning me into a piece of meat. I knew I should go to bed, but I wanted to have dinner with Greene for my picture's sake. I recognized his invitation as sincere. It was an English sequence: they invite you for a drink; if you're a dead loss they have a previous engagement; if not, you're invited to dinner. I was pleased that he hadn't flunked me.

I said, "Lead the way."

Greene went to settle the bill and ring the restaurant while I tapped a kidney in the ladies room. I met him outside the bar and said, "Bentley's – isn't that where your short story takes place?"

"Which one is that?"

"'The Invisible Japanese Gentlemen.'"

He looked a bit blank, as if he'd forgotten the story, then put on a remembering squint and said, "Oh, yes."

"One of my favorites," I said. We left the Ritz and crossed Piccadilly in the dusty mellow light that hung like lace curtains in the evening sky. Greene towered over me and I had that secure sense of protection that short people feel in the presence of much taller ones. He held my arm and steered me gallantly to Swallow Street. I knew the story well. The couple dining at Bentley's are discussing their plans: their marriage, her book. She's a bright young thing and believes her publisher's flattery – believes that she has remarkable powers of observation. Her fiancé is hopelessly in love with her, but after the meal, when he comments on the eight Japanese that have just left the restaurant, she says, "What Japanese?" and claims he doesn't love her.

I heard the waitresses muttering "Mister Greene" as we were shown to our table. Greene said, "I know what I'm having." He passed me the menu.

He began talking about trips he intended to take: Portugal, Hungary, Panama; and I wondered whether he had people joshing him and trying to persuade him to stay home. Did he have to listen to the sort of guff I had to endure? I guessed he did, even if he didn't have a Frank. I had the feeling of being with a kindred spirit, a fellow sufferer, who was completely alone, who had only his work and who, after seventy years, woke up each morning to start afresh, regarding everything he had done as more or less a failure, an inaccurate rendering of his vision, a betrayal. But I also saw how different we were: he was in his work – I wasn't in mine. And perhaps he was thinking,

"This boring little old lady only believes in right and wrong – I believe in good and evil." We were of different countries, and so our ages could never be the same. In the two hours that had passed since I had first seen Orlando in him, Greene had become more and more himself, more the complicated stranger in the fourth dimension that confounds the photograph.

"London's not what it was," he was saying. "Just around the corner one used to see tarts walking up and down. It was better then – they were all over Bayswater."

"I did some of them."

"So did I," said Greene, and passed his hand across his face as if stopping a blush. "When I was at university I used to go down to Soho, have a meal in a nice little French restaurant, a half-bottle of wine, then get myself a tart. That was very pleasant."

I didn't feel I could add anything to this.

He said, "Soho's all porno shops now. It's not erotic art. I find it brutal – there's no tenderness in it."

"It's garbage," I said. "But there's an argument in its favor."

"What's that?"

"It works," I said.

"I wouldn't know," said Greene. "I haven't seen any pornography since they legalized it."

I laughed: it was so like him. And I was annoyed that I couldn't catch that contradiction on his face. He was surprising, funny, alert, alive, a real comedian, wise and droll. Knowing that I was going to meet him for a portrait I had been faced with the dilemma that plagued me every time I set out to do someone. Against my will, I created a picture in my head beforehand and tried to imagine the shot I wanted. I had seen Greene in a bar, seedier than the one in the Ritz, a slightly angled shot with only his face in focus, and the rest – his long body, his reflective posture – dim and slightly blurred: the novelist more real than his surroundings, special and yet part of that world.

Then I saw him in the flesh, his sad heavy face, his severe mouth, his blind man's eyes, and I thought: No, a close-up with a hand on his chin – he had a watchmaker's fine hands. But his laugh changed my mind, and it struck me that it was impossible. I couldn't do him. Any portrait would freeze him, fix him, give him an eternal image, like Che looking skyward or that tubby talk-show bore everyone forgives because he was once Truman Capote, brooding under a shock of scraped-down hair.

Once, I might have taken my picture and gone, and in the printing seen his whole history in his face, past and future. Tonight, I knew despair. Photography wasn't an art, it was a craft, like making baskets. Error, the essential wrinkle in the fiber of art, was inexcusable in a craft. I had seen too much in Greene for me to be satisfied with a picture.

I said, "I think I ought to tell you that this is my last picture. I'm going to wind it up. Call it a day."

"Whatever for?"

"I'm too old to travel, for one thing."

"Which Frenchman said, 'Travel is the saddest of the pleasures'?"

"It gave me eyes."

"I understand that well enough," said Greene. "Not long ago I saw an item in a newspaper about Kim Philby."

"Always wanted to do him," I said.

"I worked for him during the war in British Intelligence. Anyway, in this item Kim said what he wanted to do more than anything else was split a bottle of wine with Graham Greene and talk over old times. I fired off a cable saying that I would meet him anywhere he named if he supplied the wine. I felt like traveling – it's as you say, an awakening. Kim cabled back, very nicely, he was busy. Some other time. I was sorry. I was quite looking forward to the trip."

"As soon as I leave home my eyes start working. I can see! It's like music – I don't really listen to it, but I can think straight while it's playing. It starts things going in my head."

Greene was listening carefully, with his fingers poised like a pianist's on the edge of the table.

"But there's something else," I said. "They're thinking of getting up a retrospective – fifty years' accumulation of pictures! I have a fella digging them out. It was his idea. I don't dare look at them – I know what they'll add up to."

"Oh?" he said, and started to smile, as if he knew what I was going to say next.

"Nothing," I said in a whisper, "nothing. They're failures, every last one of them."

"The long defeat of doing nothing well," he said, and sounded as if he was quoting. But he was still smiling. "Does that surprise you?"

"Goddamit, yes!" I said. "I don't want to be famous for something I've failed at."

"It's all failure," he said, speaking a bit too easily for my liking, as if he'd said it before and was getting so bored with it he suspected it of being untrue. Perhaps he saw my skepticism. He added, "Why else would you have started again so many times?"

I said I saw his point, but that I expected more than that from all those years of work. It was a bit late in the day to talk so easily about failure, I said, and it was obnoxious to me to realize that while I thought I had been truthful I had only been deceiving myself. I said I felt like an old fool and the worst of it was that no one else knew, and that was a sadness.

While I had been talking the food arrived. Novelists, I knew, ate what they wrote about; Greene had lemon sole and a cold bottle of Muscadet. Before he started he leaned over and took my hand gently in his. He had long fragile hands, like beautiful gloves, and a pale green ring. He held on and said, "May I ask why you're taking my picture?"

"I wanted to, and you agreed," I said nervously. "It will complete the exhibition."

"What makes you think that?"

I wanted to say a hundred things. Because we're both as old as the hills. Because you've lived a charmed life, as I have. Because no one wanted me to come to London. Because you've known what it is to be rich, famous, and misunderstood. Because anyone but me would violate you. Because you're alone, blind, betrayed, vain. Because you're happy. Because we're equals. Because you look like my poor dead brother.

"Because," I said – *because people will see my face on yours* – "it's the next best thing to taking my own picture."

I was grateful to him for not laughing at this. He said, "I'm afraid you're wrong. Deceived again, Miss Pratt. You're an original."

I said that was all very well but that I still couldn't do a self-portrait.

"Of course you can – you have," he said. "Your self-portrait will be this retrospective, not one picture, but thousands, all those photographs."

"That's what they say. I know all old people are Monday morning quarterbacks, but I also know the life I've had, and it ain't them pictures."

"No?"

"No, sir. It's all the pictures I never took. It's the circumstances."

He put his fingertips together thoughtfully, like a man preparing to pray.

"When I did Cocteau, know what he said to me? He said, 'Ja swee san doot le poet le plew incanoe et le plew celebra.' And I know goddamned well what he meant, pardon my French." I took a few mouthfuls of fish. "When I take your picture, I'm sorry, but it's not going to be you. All I can shoot is your face. If I took my own picture that's all mine would be, an old lady, looking for a house to haunt."

"With a camera," he said.

"Pardon?"

"I said, if you did your self-portrait with a camera."

"What else would I use – a monkey wrench?"

"You could do a book," he said, and dipped his prayerful hands at me as if pronouncing a blessing.

I said, "What do I know about that?"

"The less you know, the better," he said. "You have forgotten memories. What you forget becomes the compost of the imagination."

"My mulch-pile of memories."

He smiled.

"Renounce photography, the gentleman says."

"Exactly." He said it with perfect priestlike certainty.

He made it seem so simple. It was as if he had led me through a cluttered palace of regrets, from room to shadowy room, climbing stairs and kicking carpets, and when we reached the end of the darkened corridor I'd feared most he'd thrown open a door I hadn't seen and shown me air and light and empty space: hope.

"All you have to do," he said, and now he turned, "is open your eyes."

He was staring in the direction of the door.

I saw eight Japanese gentlemen gliding noiselessly in. They wore dark suits, they were small and had that deft, precisely tuned, transistorized movement. They took their places around the large table in the center of the room and sat down.

Greene said, "There's my Japanese!"

"I see them! I see them!" I said. They were angels embodying the urgent proof that I write and remember. They were Greene's own magic trick, eight creaseless Japanese conjured from thin air and seated muttering their gum-chewing language. So the evening had gone from salutation to reminiscence, subtle, solemn, funny, coincidental, and here it paused at valediction, to show my Speed Graphic as more futile than an eyeball, a box of peepstones that could only falsify this two hours. Any picture I took of Greene would be flat as a pancake. I knew that now; but I could begin again.

Greene was reddening and laughing that rich laugh, as if he was amazed by his own success, by how perfectly his trick had worked.

I said, "No one will believe this."

And, by a professional reflex, saw my angle: Greene in Bentley's; his other half on the wall mirror; the sacrificial fish staring up at him; the half-drunk bottle of wine; Greene's face animated by laughter, all his features working at once, creating light; and in the background, just visible, his triumph, the circle of Japanese, their tiny heads and neatly plastered hair. The perfect photograph pausing in a gong of light, the artist at the foreground of his own creation: Greene by Pratt.

There were tears in my eyes as I found the right f-stop and raised my Speed Graphic. I was humbled, just another crafty witness giving permanence to her piece of luck.

Greene reached over – he had very long arms – and touched the instrument. It went cold in my hands. I lowered it.

"No," he said. "Don't spoil it."

"Please."

He said, "Let this be your first memory."

"I want to do you," I said. There were tears rolling down my cheeks, but I didn't care.

"Don't you see? You've already done me."

I still held the camera in my hand. I had looped the strap over my neck. I weighed the camera, wondering what to do with it. I could barely get my breath.

"Do put it away," said Greene.

I let it drop. It jerked my head forward. I said, "I want to tell you about my brother."

"Later," he said. "Tomorrow."

In the Ritz lobby he kissed me good night. I went upstairs, and as soon as I opened the door the floor gave way under me, the ceiling caved in, and I was rolling over and over, down a long bumpy slope, dragging my heart behind me. Still tumbling I yanked the phone down by its cord and gasped into it.

Days later, a British doctor said to me, "You're a jolly lucky girl," but what I clung to was what Greene had said in the restaurant: *Let this be your first memory.*

Robert Cumming. *Academic Shading Exercise,* 1975. Gelatin silver prints.
(a) 7¹¹/₁₆ x 9⅝"; **(b)** 7⅝ x 9½". (The Museum of Modern Art, New York, purchased as the
gift of Shirley C. Burden. Copy print copyright © The Museum of Modern Art, New York)

Lies

She saw him from the back first. Even seated, he was a giant who towered over all the other students. His head was too big, his neck too thin and long, his hair almost white. She nervously rubbed her hands together and tugged her skirt straight.

"Good morning," she said. "My name is Rosemarie Hüttner. I'm a photographer, and for the next hour I'd like to tell you something about portrait photography."

The students eyed her wearily. Several yawned in her face, one girl was knitting, only the giant looked at her expectantly, even gave her a smile. But it wrenched his face into a grimace, his mouth twitched, and one eye rolled about out of control. Everything about his face was wrong. It looked like patches sewn together – but not because of a bad accident, the whole head was too misshapen for that, the brow too high and wide. Like a hydrocephalic, Rosemarie thought, that might well be it. She tried not to stare at him, but he was sitting right in the middle of the room, with his white hair and his chalky pale skin.

She spoke about light.

"The first thing the eye always notices is the brightest spot on a photograph. You need to be aware of that before composing a picture."

The giant must have wandered in here by mistake, and she braced herself for him to start babbling wildly to himself. The students paid him as little attention as they did her. Their curiosity about their new teacher sputtered out within a few seconds. Only he seemed to listen attentively, hanging on her words with one eye, the other wandering askew.

Rosemarie pulled from her pocket a light bulb on a cord.

"I'd like to try a little experiment with you," she announced with forced enthusiasm. "I'll need a volunteer to come up front here." Before she even finished her sentence, she knew what she was afraid of. And, sure enough, the giant rose clumsily to his feet and walked slowly toward her. The arms dangled like little appendages from his enormous body; he walked with knees slightly bent, carefully setting one foot in front of the other. "Maybe it'd be better," she said hastily, "if we started with a female face." What a stupid ploy, she thought. The giant stopped in his tracks, wrenched his face into another smile, slowly turned around, and went back to his seat. Then came a long pause. The students watched her for what would happen next. Rosemarie's armpits started itching. She pointed to a girl of average prettiness, who reluctantly stood up.

Rosemarie let down the blinds and switched on the light bulb.

"You will now see how her expression changes depending on how I direct the source of light onto her face."

She wandered with her light bulb around the girl's face, making it beautiful. The brow was a little too low – she made it disappear in darkness. She accentuated the classic straight nose, let a dimple cast a strong shadow.

"Photography has nothing to do with truth. The camera lies, and it's up to you how you let it lie. And you use light to do the lying." She held the light bulb under the girl's chin, which made the face hard, bitter, and old.

"Never try to be objective. Objectivity is for the timid and half-hearted. Objectivity wants to be universal. The more subjective you are, however, the greater success you'll have in expressing something universal and valid."

She thanked the girl and was just about to turn around and pull up the blinds, when the giant stood up again and moved resolutely toward her. She gesticulated helplessly with the light bulb, but simply couldn't come up with a new excuse. In the semi-darkness she saw her students shift expectantly in their seats. I can't, I simply can't, she thought. He calmly sat down in front of the class and looked eagerly at her. Then he nodded. Her heart was pounding as she tentatively raised the light bulb and directed it onto his face – which promptly shattered into monstrous details, the gigantic brow looming white, the distance between the eyes so large now that one eye no longer seemed to have anything to do with the other. Terrified, she lowered the bulb. Use light to lie, use light to lie, she muttered to herself in a monotone.

She lifted the bulb high above his head to light it from the rear, and turned him into a madman with a halo. He went right on staring at her with the same imbecilic grin. She desperately tried to remember all her professional tricks for emphasizing a face's beauty and distinctive traits and allowing the rest to vanish in gracious darkness. But no matter where she looked in that face, she found nothing she could have used to make the rest forgettable – every inch of this mass of flesh betrayed the whole.

She covered the beam with her hand, let it skitter over his face, and succeeded only in creating one new monster after the other. Sweat streamed down her body. She had made fat politicians look distinguished, had turned old actresses young, had restored inspiration to drunken artists. Her light had lied with a vengeance, and now she couldn't persuade it to tell one tiny fib. The "Queen of Light and Shadow," a newspaper had once called her – but the fluorescent light in the bare room had dealt with him more kindly than she.

She stood there rigid, the light bulb raised high in her hand. Turning toward her in surprise, he projected an oversized shadow on the wall, a profile so lacking in anything human it was like a great beast. She was shaking as she pulled the plug out of the wall socket. He said a soft "Thanks" into the darkness. She was considering making a dash for it, but then a student raised the blinds.

She couldn't recall later how she had got through that hour. Mute and disdainful, so it seemed to her, the students gathered up their books and notes and left the room.

She packed up her light bulb and cursed it. He stood in the door, blocking her way. She looked up at him.

"May I ask you something?" he said in a soft, very gentle voice. She nodded, amazed that he could speak at all.

"If someone were to tell you that he would like to become a photographer, but was terribly afraid of asking people if he could photograph them, what advice would you give him?" After a pause he added, "I presume you know who I'm talking about. Might I invite you to join me in a cup of coffee?"

He very carefully balanced the coffee on a tray as he moved ahead of her through the student dining hall, and Rosemarie sensed how the eyes of all the students were following their progress. She automatically took a chair on the side of the table that lay in shadows, and was immediately sorry she had. The giant sat down opposite her, and one of those lamps with a plastic orange shade, the kind you see in every coffee shop, shone mercilessly in his face. He watched her, biding his time and stirring his coffee, slowly, ever so slowly. The spoon looked tiny in his gigantic hand. She did not look at him when she finally began to speak. "Everyone has fears," she said quickly. "And if I had no fears, I wouldn't take pictures. I started taking them to overcome my fear."

"What are you afraid of?" he asked amiably, laying his thick white hands on the table. All his movements were so deliberate they seemed to occur in slow motion.

"Oh, of . . . of the world. Especially of things I don't know. I photograph them so that I can get to know them and that way I don't have to be afraid of them anymore." Rosemarie could not recall ever having described her profession so clearly, even to herself.

"And? Does that work?" he asked gently.

"No," she said. And he began to laugh, and his whole face quivered and wobbled with delight. He snorted, tears of laughter zigzagging down his distorted face. Finally he managed to say, "So there's really no point in it?"

"No, not really. But while you're doing it, you always think it might work."

Still smiling, he took her hands in his. They were very warm and soft, like two big pillows. "You shouldn't be such a pessimist," he said, and bent toward her. "Afraid of the world – well, if that's all." The lamp above the table shone on his ears. He had small, well-shaped ears, the prettiest ears she had ever seen.

Blow-Up

JULIO CORTÁZAR

It'll never be known how this has to be told, in the first person or in the second, using the third-person plural or continually inventing modes that will serve for nothing. If one might say: I will see the moon rose, or: we hurt me at the back of my eyes, and especially: you the blond woman was the clouds that race before my your his our yours their faces. What the hell.

Seated ready to tell it, if one might go to drink a bock over there, and the typewriter continue by itself (because I use the machine), that would be perfection. And that's not just a manner of speaking. Perfection, yes, because here is the aperture which must be counted also as a machine (of another sort, a Contax 1.1.2) and it is possible that one machine may know more about another machine than I, you, she – the blond – and the clouds. But I have the dumb luck to know that if I go this Remington will sit turned to stone on top of the table with the air of being twice as quiet that mobile things have when they are not moving. So, I have to write. One of us all has to write, if this is going to get told. Better that it be me who am dead, for I'm less compromised than the rest; I who see only the clouds and can think without being distracted, write without being distracted (there goes another, with a gray edge) and remember without being distracted, I who am dead (and I'm alive, I'm not trying to fool anybody, you'll see when we get to the moment, because I have to begin some way and I've begun with this period, the last one back, the one at the beginning, which in the end is the best of the periods when you want to tell something).

All of a sudden I wonder why I have to tell this, but if one begins to wonder why he does all he does do, if one wonders why he accepts an invitation to lunch (now a pigeon's flying by and it seems to me a sparrow), or why when someone has told us a good joke immediately there starts up something like a tickling in the stomach and we are not at peace until we've gone into the office across the hall and told the joke over again; then it feels good immediately, one is fine, happy, and can get back to work. For I imagine that no one has explained this, that really the best thing is to put aside all decorum and tell it, because, after all's done, nobody is ashamed of breathing or of putting on his shoes; they're things that you do, and when something weird happens, when you find a spider in your shoe or if you take a breath and feel like a broken window, then you have to tell what's happening, tell it to the guys at the office or to the doctor. Oh, doctor, every time I take a breath . . . Always tell it, always get rid of that tickle in the stomach that bothers you.

And now that we're finally going to tell it, let's put things a little bit in order, we'd be walking down the staircase in this house as far as Sunday, November 7, just a month back. One goes down five floors and stands then in the Sunday in the sun one would not have suspected of Paris in November, with a large appetite to walk around, to see things, to take photos (because we were photographers, I'm a photographer). I know that the most difficult thing is going to be finding a way to tell it, and I'm not afraid of repeating myself. It's going to be difficult because nobody really knows who it is telling it, if I am I or what actually occurred or what I'm seeing (clouds, and once in a while a pigeon) or if, simply, I'm telling a truth which is only my truth, and then is the truth only for my stomach, for this impulse to go running out and to finish up in some manner with, this, whatever it is.

We're going to tell it slowly, what happens in the middle of what I'm writing is coming already. If they replace me, if, so soon, I don't know what to say, if the clouds stop coming and something else starts (because it's impossible that this keep coming, clouds passing continually and occasionally a pigeon), if something out of all this . . . And after the "if" what am I going to put if I'm going to close the sentence structure correctly? But if I begin to ask questions, I'll never tell anything, maybe to tell would be like an answer, at least for someone who's reading it.

Roberto Michel, French-Chilean, translator and in his spare time an amateur photographer, left number 11, rue Monsieur-le-Prince Sunday November 7 of the current year (now there're two small ones passing, with silver linings). He had spent three weeks working on the French version of a treatise on challenges and appeals by José Norberto Allende, professor at the University of Santiago. It's rare that there's wind in Paris, and even more seldom a wind like this that swirled around corners and rose up to whip at old wooden venetian blinds behind which astonished ladies commented variously on how unreliable the weather had been these last few years. But the sun was out also, riding the wind and friend of the cats, so there was nothing that would keep me from taking a walk along the docks of the Seine and taking photos of the Conservatoire and Sainte-Chapelle. It was hardly ten o'clock, and I figured that by eleven the light would be good, the best you can get in the fall; to kill some time I detoured around by the Île Saint-Louis and started to walk along the quai d'Anjou, I stared for a bit at the Hôtel de Lauzun, I recited bits from Apollinaire which always get into my head when I pass in front of the Hôtel de Lauzun (and at that I ought to be remembering the other poet, but Michel is an obstinate beggar), and when the wind stopped all at once and the sun came out at least twice as hard (I mean warmer, but really it's the same thing), I sat down on the parapet and felt terribly happy in the Sunday morning.

One of the many ways of contesting level zero, and one of the best, is to take photographs, an activity in which one should start becoming an adept very early in life, teach it to children since it requires discipline, aesthetic education, a good eye and steady fingers. I'm not talking about waylaying the lie like any old reporter, snapping the stupid silhouette of the VIP leaving number 10 Downing Street, but in all ways when one is walking about with a camera, one has almost a duty to be attentive, to not lose that abrupt and happy rebound of sun's rays off an old stone, or the pigtails-flying run of a small girl going home with a loaf of bread or a bottle of milk. Michel knew that the photographer always worked as a permutation of his personal way of seeing the world as other than the camera insidiously imposed upon it (now a large cloud is going by, almost black), but he lacked no confidence in himself, knowing that he had only to go out without the Contax to recover the keynote of distraction, the sight without a frame around it, light without the diaphragm aperture or 1/250 sec. Right now (what a word, *now*, what a dumb lie) I was able to sit quietly on the railing overlooking the river watching the red-and-black motorboats passing below without it occurring to me to think photographically of the scenes, nothing more than letting myself go in the letting go of objects, running immobile in the stream of time. And then the wind was not blowing.

After, I wandered down the quai de Bourbon to the end of the isle where the intimate square was (intimate because it was small, not that it was hidden, offering its whole breast to the river and the sky), and I enjoyed it, a lot. Nothing there but a couple and, of course, pigeons; maybe even some of those which are flying past now so that I'm seeing them. A leap up and I settled on the wall, and let myself turn about and be caught and fixed by the sun, giving it my face and ears and hands (I kept my gloves in my pocket). I had no desire to shoot pictures, and lit a cigarette to be doing something; I think it was that moment when the match was about to touch the tobacco that I saw the young boy for the first time.

What I'd thought was a couple seemed much more now a boy with his mother, although at the same time I realized that it was not a kid and his mother, and that it was a couple in the sense that we always allege to couples when we see them leaning up against the parapets or embracing on the benches in the squares. As I had nothing else to do, I had more than enough time to wonder why the boy was so nervous, like a young colt or a hare, sticking his hands into his pockets, taking them out immediately, one after the other, running his fingers through his hair, changing his stance, and especially why was he afraid, well, you could guess that from every gesture, a fear suffocated by his shyness, an impulse to step backward which he telegraphed, his body standing as if it were on the edge of flight, holding itself back in a final, pitiful decorum.

All this was so clear, ten feet away – and we were alone against the parapet at the tip of the island – that at the beginning the boy's fright didn't let me see the blond very well. Now, thinking back on it, I see her much better at that first second when I read her face (she'd turned around suddenly, swinging like a metal weathercock, and the eyes, the eyes were there), when I vaguely understood what might have been occurring to the boy and figured it would be worth the trouble to stay and watch (the wind was blowing their words away and they were speaking in a low murmur). I think that I know how to look, if it's something I know, and also that every looking oozes with mendacity, because it's that which expels us furthest outside ourselves, without the least guarantee, whereas to smell, or (but Michel rambles on to himself easily enough, there's no need to let him harangue on this way). In any case, if the likely inaccuracy can be seen beforehand, it becomes possible again to look; perhaps it suffices to choose between looking and the reality looked at, to strip things of all their unnecessary clothing. And surely all that is difficult besides.

As for the boy I remember the image before his actual body (that will clear itself up later), while now I am sure that I remember the woman's body much better than the image. She was thin and willowy, two unfair words to describe what she was, and was wearing an almost black fur coat, almost long, almost handsome. All the morning's wind (now it was hardly a breeze and it wasn't cold) had blown through her blond hair, which pared away her white, bleak face – two unfair words – and put the world at her feet and horribly alone in front of her dark eyes, her eyes fell on things like two eagles, two leaps into nothingness, two puffs of green slime. I'm not describing anything, it's more a matter of trying to understand it. And I said two puffs of green slime.

Let's be fair, the boy was well enough dressed and was sporting yellow gloves which I would have sworn belonged to his older brother, a student of law or sociology; it was pleasant to see the fingers of the gloves sticking out of his jacket pocket. For a long time I didn't see his face, barely a profile, not stupid – a terrified bird, a Fra Filippo angel, rice pudding with milk – and the back of an adolescent who wants to take up judo and has had a scuffle or two in defense of an idea or his sister. Turning fourteen, perhaps fifteen, one would guess that he was dressed and fed by his parents but without a nickel in his pocket, having to debate with his buddies before making up his mind to buy a coffee, a cognac, a pack of cigarettes. He'd walk through the streets thinking of the girls in his class, about how good it would be to go to the movies and see the latest film, or to buy novels or neckties or bottles of liquor with green-and-white labels on them. At home (it would be a respectable home, lunch at noon and romantic landscapes on the walls, with a dark entryway and a mahogany umbrella stand inside the door) there'd be the slow rain of time, for studying, for being mama's hope, for looking like dad, for writing to his aunt in Avignon. So that there was a lot of walking the streets, the whole of the river for him (but without a nickel) and the mysterious city of fifteen-year-olds with its signs in doorways, its terrifying cats, a paper of fried potatoes for thirty francs, the pornographic magazine folded four ways, a solitude like the emptiness of his pockets, the eagerness for so much that was incomprehensible but illumined by a total love, by the availability analogous to the wind and the streets.

This biography was of the boy and of any boy whatsoever, but this particular one now, you could see he was insular, surrounded solely by the blond's presence as she continued talking with him. (I'm tired of insisting, but two long ragged ones just went by. That morning I don't think I looked at the sky once, because what was happening with the boy and the woman appeared so soon I could do nothing but look at them and wait, look at them and . . .) To cut it short, the boy was agitated and one could guess without too much trouble what had just occurred a few minutes before, at most half an hour. The boy had come onto the tip of the island, seen the woman and thought her marvelous. The woman was waiting for that because she was there waiting for that, or maybe the boy arrived before her and she saw him from one of the balconies or from a car and got out to meet him, starting the conversation with whatever, from the beginning she was sure that he was going to be afraid and want to run off, and that, naturally, he'd stay, stiff and sullen, pretending experience and the pleasure of the adventure. The rest was easy because it was happening ten feet away from me, and anyone could have gauged the stages of the game, the derisive, competitive fencing; its major attraction was not that it was happening but in foreseeing its denouement. The boy would try to end it by pretending a date, an obligation, whatever, and would go stumbling off disconcerted, wishing he were walking with some assurance, but naked under the mocking glance which would follow him until he was out of sight. Or rather, he would stay there, fascinated or simply incapable of taking the initiative, and the woman would begin to touch his face gently, muss his hair, still talking to him voicelessly, and soon would take him by the arm to lead him off, unless he, with an uneasiness beginning to tinge the edge of desire, even his stake in the adventure, would rouse himself to put his arm around her waist and to kiss her. Any of this could have happened, though it did not, and perversely Michel waited, sitting on the railing, making the settings almost without looking at the camera, ready to take a picturesque shot of a corner of the island with an uncommon couple talking and looking at one another.

Strange how the scene (almost nothing: two figures there mismatched in their youth) was taking on a disquieting aura. I thought it was I imposing it, and that my photo, if I shot it, would reconstitute things in their true stupidity. I would have liked to know what he was thinking, a man in a gray hat sitting at the wheel of a car parked on the dock which led up to the footbridge, and whether he was reading the paper or asleep. I had just discovered him because people inside a parked car have a tendency to disappear, they get lost in that wretched, private cage stripped of the beauty that motion and danger give it. And nevertheless, the car had been there the whole time, forming part (or deforming that part) of the isle. A car: like saying a lighted streetlamp, a park bench. Never like saying wind, sunlight, those elements always new to the skin and the eyes, and also the boy and the woman, unique, put there to change the island, to show it to me in another way. Finally, it may have been that the man with the newspaper also became aware of what was happening and would, like me, feel that malicious sensation of waiting for everything to happen. Now the woman had swung around smoothly, putting the young boy between herself and the wall, I saw them almost in profile, and he was taller, though not much taller, and yet she dominated him, it seemed like she was hovering over him (her laugh, all at once, a whip of feathers), crushing him just by being there, smiling, one hand taking a stroll through the air. Why wait any longer? Aperture at sixteen, a sighting which would not include the horrible black car, but yes, that tree, necessary to break up too much gray space . . .

I raised the camera, pretended to study a focus that did not include them, and waited and watched closely, sure that I would finally catch the revealing expression, one that would sum it all up, life that is rhythmed by movement but which a stiff image destroys, taking time in cross-section, if we do not choose the essential imperceptible fraction of it. I did not have to wait long. The woman was getting on with the job of handcuffing the boy smoothly, stripping from him what was left of his freedom a hair at a time, in an incredibly slow and delicious torture. I imagined the possible endings (now a small fluffy cloud appears, almost alone in the sky), I saw their arrival at the house (a basement apartment probably, which she would have filled with large cushions and cats) and conjectured the boy's terror and his desperate decision to play it cool and to be led off pretending there was nothing new in it for him. Closing my eyes, if I did in fact close my eyes, I set the scene: the teasing kisses, the woman mildly repelling the hands that were trying to undress her, like in novels, on a bed that would have a lilac-colored comforter, on the other hand she taking off his clothes, plainly mother and son under a milky yellow light, and everything would end up as usual, perhaps, but maybe everything would go otherwise, and the initiation of the adolescent would not happen, she would not let it happen, after a long prologue wherein the awkwardnesses, the exasperating caresses, the running of hands over bodies would be resolved in who knows what, in a separate and solitary pleasure, in a petulant denial mixed with the art of tiring and disconcerting so much poor innocence. It might go like that, it might very well go like that; that woman was not looking for the boy as a lover, and at the same time she was dominating him toward some end impossible to understand if you do not imagine it as a cruel game, the desire to desire without satisfaction, to excite herself for someone else, someone who in no way could be that kid.

Michel is guilty of making literature, of indulging in fabricated unrealities. Nothing pleases him more than to imagine exceptions to the rule, individuals outside the species, not-always-repugnant monsters. But that woman invited speculation, perhaps giving clues enough for the fantasy to hit the bull's-eye. Before she left, and now that she would fill my imaginings for several days, for I'm given to ruminating, I decided not to lose a moment more. I got it all into the viewfinder (with the tree, the railing, the eleven-o'clock sun) and took the shot. In time to realize that they both had noticed and stood there looking at me, the boy surprised and as though questioning, but she was irritated, her face and body flat-footedly hostile, feeling robbed, ignominiously recorded on a small chemical image.

I might be able to tell it in much greater detail but it's not worth the trouble. The woman said that no one had the right to take a picture without permission, and demanded that I hand her over the film. All this in a dry, clear voice with a good Parisian accent, which rose in color and tone with every phrase. For my part, it hardly mattered whether she got the roll of film or not, but anyone who knows me will tell you, if you want anything from me, ask nicely. With the result that I restricted myself to formulating the opinion that not only was photography in public places not prohibited, but it was looked upon with decided favor, both private and official. And while that was getting said, I noticed on the sly how the boy was falling back, sort of actively backing up though without moving, and all at once (it seemed almost incredible) he turned and broke into a run, the poor kid, thinking that he was walking off and in fact in full flight, running past the side of the car, disappearing like a gossamer filament of angel-spit in the morning air.

But filaments of angel-spittle are also called devil-spit and Michel had to endure rather particular curses, to hear himself called meddler and imbecile, taking great pains meanwhile to smile and to abate with simple movements of his head such a hard sell. As I was beginning to get tired, I heard the car door slam. The man in the gray hat was there, looking at us. It was only at that point that I realized he was playing a part in the comedy.

He began to walk toward us, carrying in his hand the paper he had been pretending to read. What I remember best is the grimace that twisted his mouth askew, it covered his face with wrinkles, changed somewhat both in location and shape because his lips trembled and the grimace went from one side of his mouth to the other as though it were on wheels, independent and involuntary. But the rest stayed fixed, a flour-powdered clown or bloodless man, dull dry skin, eyes deep-set, the nostrils black and prominently visible, blacker than the eyebrows or hair or the black necktie. Walking cautiously as though the pavement hurt his feet; I saw patent-leather shoes with such thin soles that he must have felt every roughness in the pavement. I don't know why I got down off the railing or very well why I decided to not give them the photo, to refuse that demand in which I guessed at their fear and cowardice. The clown and the woman consulted each other in silence: we made a perfect and unbearable triangle, something I felt compelled to break with a crack of a whip. I laughed in their faces and began to walk off, a little more slowly, I imagine, than the boy. At the level of the first houses, beside the iron footbridge, I turned around to look at them. They were not moving, but the man had dropped his newspaper; it seemed to me that the woman, her back to the parapet, ran her hands over the stone with the classical and absurd gesture of someone pursued looking for a way out.

What happened after that happened here, almost just now, in a room on the fifth floor. Several days went by before Michel developed the photos he'd taken on Sunday; his shots of the Conservatoire and Sainte-Chapelle were all they should be. Then he found two or three proof shots he'd forgotten, a poor attempt to catch a cat perched astonishingly on the roof of a rambling public urinal, and also the shot of the blond and the kid. The negative was so good that he made an enlargement; the enlargement was so good that he made one very much larger, almost the size of a poster. It did not occur to him (now one wonders and wonders) that only the shots of the Conservatoire were worth so much work. Of the whole series, the snapshot of the tip of the island was the only one that interested him; he tacked up the enlargement on one wall of the room, and the first day he spent some time looking at it and remembering, that gloomy operation of comparing the memory with the gone reality; a frozen memory, like any photo, where nothing is missing, not even, and especially, nothingness, the true solidifier of the scene. There was the woman, there was the boy, the tree rigid above their heads, the sky as sharp as the stone of the parapet, clouds and stones melded into a single substance and inseparable (now one with sharp edges is going by, like a thunderhead). The first two days I accepted what I had done, from the photo itself to the enlargement on the wall, and didn't even question that every once in a while I would interrupt my translation of José Norberto Allende's treatise to encounter once more the woman's face, the dark splotches on the railing. I'm such a jerk; it had never occurred to me that when we look at a photo from the front, the eyes reproduce exactly the position and the vision of the lens; it's these things that are taken for granted and it never occurs to anyone to think about them. From my chair, with the type-writer directly in front of me, I looked at the photo ten feet away, and then it occurred to me that I had hung it exactly at the point of view of the lens. It looked very good that way; no doubt, it was the best way to appreciate a photo, though the angle from the diagonal doubt-less has its pleasures and might even divulge different aspects. Every few minutes, for example when I was unable to find the way to say in good French what José Norberto Allende was saying in very good Spanish, I raised my eyes and looked at the photo; sometimes the woman would catch my eye, sometimes the boy, sometimes the pavement where a dry leaf had fallen admirably situated to heighten a lateral section. Then I rested a bit from my labors, and I enclosed myself again happily in that morning in which the photo was drenched, I recalled ironically the angry picture of the woman demanding I give her the photograph, the boy's pathetic and ridiculous flight, the entrance on the scene of the man with the white face. Basically, I was satisfied with myself; my part had not been too brilliant, and since the French have been given the gift of the sharp response, I did not see very well why I'd chosen to leave without a complete demonstration of the rights, privileges, and prerogatives of citizens. The important thing, the really important thing, was having helped the kid escape in time (this in case my theorizing was correct, which was not sufficiently proven, but the running away itself seemed to show it so). Out of plain meddling, I had given him the opportunity finally to take advantage of his fright to do something useful; now he would be regretting it, feeling his honor impaired, his manhood diminished. That was better than the attentions of a woman capable of looking as she had looked at him on that island. Michel is something of a puritan at times, he believes that one should not seduce someone from a position of strength. In the last analysis, taking that photo had been a good act.

Well, it wasn't because of the good act that I looked at it between paragraphs while I was working. At that moment I didn't know the reason, the reason I had tacked the enlargement onto the wall; maybe all fatal acts happen that way, and that is the condition of their fulfillment. I don't think the almost furtive trembling of the leaves on the tree alarmed me, I was working on a sentence and rounded it out successfully. Habits are like immense herbariums, in the end an enlargement of 32 x 28 looks like a movie screen, where, on the tip of the island, a woman is speaking with a boy and a tree is shaking its dry leaves over their heads.

But her hands were just too much. I had just translated: "In that case, the second key resides in the intrinsic nature of difficulties which societies . . ." – when I saw the woman's hand beginning to stir slowly, finger by finger. There was nothing left of me, a phrase in French which I would never have to finish, a typewriter on the floor, a chair that squeaked and shook, fog. The kid had ducked his head like boxers do when they've done all they can and are waiting for the final blow to fall; he had turned up the collar of his overcoat and seemed more a prisoner than ever, the perfect victim helping promote the catastrophe. Now the woman was talking into his ear, and her hand opened again to lay itself against his cheekbone, to caress and caress it, burning it, taking her time. The kid was less startled than he was suspicious, once or twice he poked his head over the woman's shoulder and she continued talking, saying something that made him look back every few minutes toward that area where Michel knew the car was parked and the man in the gray hat, carefully eliminated from the photo but present in the boy's eyes (how doubt that now), in the words of the woman, in the woman's hands, in the vicarious presence of the woman. When I saw the man come up, stop near them and look at them, his hands in his pockets and a stance somewhere between disgusted and demanding, the master who is about to whistle in his dog after a frolic in the square, I understood, if that was to understand, what had to happen now, what had to have happened then, what would have to happen at that moment, among these people, just where I had poked my nose in to upset an established order, interfering innocently in that which had not happened, but which was now going to happen, now was going to be fulfilled. And what I had imagined earlier was much less horrible than the reality, that woman, who was not there by herself, she was not caressing or propositioning or encouraging for her own pleasure, to lead the angel away with his tousled hair and play the tease with his terror and his eager grace. The real boss was waiting there, smiling petulantly, already certain of the business; he was not the first to send a woman in the vanguard, to bring him the prisoners manacled with flowers. The rest of it would be so simple, the car, some house or another, drinks, stimulating engravings, tardy tears, the awakening in hell. And there was nothing I could do, this time I could do absolutely nothing. My strength had been a photograph, that, there, where they were taking their revenge on me, demonstrating clearly what was going to happen. The photo had been taken, the time had run out, gone; we were so far from one another, the abusive act had certainly already taken place, the tears already shed and the rest conjecture and sorrow. All at once the order was inverted, they were alive, moving, they were deciding and had decided, they were going to their future; and I on this side, prisoner of another time, in a room on the fifth floor, to not know who they were, that woman, that man, and that boy, to be only the lens of my camera, something fixed, rigid, incapable of intervention. It was horrible, their mocking me, deciding it before my impotent eye, mocking me, for the boy again was looking at the flour-faced clown and I had to accept the fact that he was going to say yes, that the proposition carried money with it or a gimmick, and I couldn't yell for him to run, or even open the road to him again with a new photo, a small and almost meek intervention which would ruin the framework of drool and perfume. Everything was going to resolve itself right there, at that moment; there was like an immense silence which had nothing to do with physical silence. It was stretching it out, setting itself up. I think I screamed, I screamed terribly and at that exact second I realized I was beginning to move toward them, four inches, a step, another step, the tree swung its branches rhythmically in the foreground, a place where the railing was tarnished emerged from the frame, the woman's face turned toward me as though surprised, was enlarging, and then I turned a bit, I mean that the camera turned a little, and without losing sight of the woman, I began to close in on the man who was looking at me with the black holes he had in place of eyes, surprised and angered both, he looked, wanting to nail me onto the air, and at that instant I happened to see something like a large bird outside the focus that was flying in a single swoop in front of the picture, and I leaned up against the wall of my room and was happy because the boy had just managed to escape, I saw him running off, in focus again, sprinting with his hair flying in the wind, learning finally to fly across the island, to arrive at the footbridge, return to the city. For the second time he'd escaped them, for the second time I was helping him escape, returning him to his precarious paradise. Out of breath, I stood in front of them; no need to step closer, the game was played out. Of the woman you could see just maybe a shoulder and a bit of the hair, brutally cut off by the frame of the picture; but the man was directly center, his mouth half open, you could see a shaking black tongue, and he lifted his hands slowly, bringing them into the foreground, an instant still in perfect focus, and then all of him a lump that blotted out the island, the tree, and I shut my eyes, I didn't want to see any more, and I covered my face and broke into tears like an idiot.

Now there's a big white cloud, as on all these days, all this untellable time. What remains to be said is always a cloud, two clouds, or long hours of a sky perfectly clear, a very clean, clear rectangle tacked up with pins on the wall of my room. That was what I saw when I opened my eyes and dried them with my fingers: the clear sky, and then a cloud that drifted in from the left, passed gracefully and slowly across and disappeared on the right. And then another, and for a change sometimes, everything gets gray, all one enormous cloud, and suddenly the splotches of rain cracking down, for a long spell you can see it raining over the picture, like a spell of weeping reversed, and little by little, the frame becomes clear, perhaps the sun comes out, and again the clouds begin to come, two at a time, three at a time. And the pigeons once in a while, and a sparrow or two.

The Adventures of

a Photographer

ITALO CALVINO

When spring comes, the city's inhabitants, by the hundreds of thousands, go out on Sundays with leather cases over their shoulders. And
they photograph one another. They come back as happy as hunters
with bulging game bags; they spend days waiting, with sweet anxiety,
to see the developed pictures (anxiety to which some add the subtle
pleasure of alchemistic manipulations in the darkroom, forbidding
any intrusion by members of the family, relishing the acid smell that
is harsh to the nostrils). It is only when they have the photos before
their eyes that they seem to take tangible possession of the day they
spent, only then that the mountain stream, the movement of the
child with his pail, the glint of the sun on the wife's legs take on the
irrevocability of what has been and can no longer be doubted.
Everything else can drown in the unreliable shadow of memory.

Seeing a good deal of his friends and colleagues, Antonio Paraggi,
a nonphotographer, sensed a growing isolation. Every week he discovered that the conversations of those who praise the sensitivity of a
filter or discourse on the number of DINs were swelled by the voice
of yet another to whom he had confided until yesterday, convinced
that they were shared, his sarcastic remarks about an activity that
to him seemed so unexciting, so lacking in surprises. Professionally,

133

Antonino Paraggi occupied an executive position in the distribution
department of a production firm, but his real passion was comment-
ing to his friends on current events large and small, unraveling the
thread of general causes from the tangle of details; in short, by men-
tal attitude he was a philosopher, and he devoted all his thoroughness
to grasping the significance of even the events most remote from his
own experience. Now he felt that something in the essence of photographic man was eluding him, the secret appeal that made new
adepts continue to join the ranks of the amateurs of the lens, some
boasting of the progress of their technical and artistic skill, others, on
the contrary, giving all the credit to the efficiency of the camera they
had purchased, which was capable (according to them) of producing
masterpieces even when operated by inept hands (as they declared
their own to be, because wherever pride aimed at magnifying the vir-
tues of mechanical devices, subjective talent accepted a proportionate
humiliation). Antonino Paraggi understood that neither the one nor
the other motive of satisfaction was decisive: the secret lay elsewhere.

It must be said that his examination of photography to discover
the causes of a private dissatisfaction – as of someone who feels
excluded from something – was to a certain extent a trick Antonino
played on himself, to avoid having to consider another, more evident,
process that was separating him from his friends. What was happening was this: his acquaintances, of his age, were all getting married,
one after another, and starting families, while Antonino remained a
bachelor. Yet between the two phenomena there was undoubtedly a
connection, inasmuch as the passion for the lens often develops in a
natural, virtually physiological way as a secondary effect of fatherhood. One of the first instincts of parents, after they have brought a
child into the world, is to photograph it. Given the speed of growth,
it becomes necessary to photograph the child often, because nothing
is more fleeting and unmemorable than a six-month-old infant, soon
deleted and replaced by one of eight months, and then one of a year;

and all the perfection that, to the eyes of parents, a child of three may have reached cannot prevent its being destroyed by that of the four-year-old. The photograph album remains the only place where all these fleeting perfections are saved and juxtaposed, each aspiring to an incomparable absoluteness of its own. In the passion of new parents for framing their offspring in the sights to reduce them to the immobility of black-and-white or a full-color slide, the nonphotographer and nonprocreator Antonino saw chiefly a phase in the race toward madness lurking in that black instrument. But his reflections on the iconography-family-madness nexus were summary and reticent: otherwise he would have realized that the person actually running the greatest risk was himself, the bachelor.

In the circle of Antonino's friends, it was customary to spend the weekend out of town, in a group, following a tradition that for many of them dated back to their student days and that had been extended to include their girlfriends, then their wives and their children, as well as wet nurses and governesses, and in some cases in-laws and new acquaintances of both sexes. But since the continuity of their habits, their getting together, had never lapsed, Antonino could pretend that nothing had changed with the passage of the years and that they were still the band of young men and women of the old days, rather than a conglomerate of families in which he remained the only surviving bachelor.

More and more often, on these excursions to the sea or the mountains, when it came time for the family group or the multifamily picture, an outsider was asked to lend a hand, a passer-by perhaps, willing to press the button of the camera already focused and aimed in the desired direction. In these cases, Antonino couldn't refuse his services: he would take the camera from the hands of a father or a mother, who would then run to assume his or her place in the second row, sticking his head forward between two other heads, or crouching among the little ones; and Antonino, concentrating all his strength in the finger destined for this use, would press. The first times, an awkward stiffening of his arm would make the lens veer to capture the masts of ships or the spires of steeples, or to decapitate grandparents, uncles, and aunts. He was accused of doing this on purpose, reproached for making a joke in poor taste. It wasn't true: his intention was to lend the use of his finger as docile instrument of the collective wish, but also to exploit his temporary position of privilege to admonish both photographers and their subjects as to the significance of their actions. As soon as the pad of his finger reached the desired condition of detachment from the rest of his person and personality, he was free to communicate his theories in well-reasoned discourse, framing at the same time well-composed little groups. (A few accidental successes had sufficed to give him nonchalance and assurance with viewfinders and light meters.)

"... Because once you've begun," he would preach, "there is no reason why you should stop. The line between the reality that is photographed because it seems beautiful to us and the reality that seems beautiful because it has been photographed is very narrow. If you take a picture of Pierluca because he's building a sand castle, there is no reason not to take his picture while he's crying because the castle has collapsed, and then while the nurse consoles him by helping him find a sea shell in the sand. The minute you start saying something, 'Ah, how beautiful! We must photograph it!' you are already close to the view of the person who thinks that everything that is not photographed is lost, as if it had never existed, and that therefore, in order really to live, you must photograph as much as you can, and to photograph as much as you can you must either live in the most photographable way possible, or else consider photographable every moment of your life. The first course leads to stupidity; the second to madness."

"You're the one who's mad and stupid," his friends would say to him, "and a pain in the ass, into the bargain."

"For the person who wants to capture everything that passes before his eyes," Antonino would explain, even if nobody was listening to him any more, "the only coherent way to act is to snap at least one picture a minute, from the instant he opens his eyes in the morning to when he goes to sleep. This is the only way that the rolls of exposed film will represent a faithful diary of our days, with nothing left out. If I were to start taking pictures, I'd see this thing through, even if it meant losing my mind. But the rest of you still insist on making a choice. What sort of choice? A choice in the idyllic sense, apologetic, consolatory, at peace with nature, the fatherland, the family. Your choice isn't only photographic; it is a choice of life, which leads you to exclude dramatic conflicts, the knots of contradiction, the great tensions of will, passion, aversion. So you think you are saving yourselves from madness, but you are falling into mediocrity, into hebetude."

A girl named Bice, someone's ex-sister-in-law, and another named Lydia, someone else's ex-secretary, asked him please to take a snapshot of them while they were playing ball among the waves. He consented, but since in the meanwhile he had worked out a theory in opposition to snapshots, he dutifully expressed it to the two friends:

"What drives you two girls to cut from the mobile continuum of your day these temporal slices, the thickness of a second? Tossing the ball back and forth, you are living in the present, but the moment the scansion of the frames is insinuated between your acts it is no longer the pleasure of the game that motivates you but, rather, that of seeing yourselves again in the future, of rediscovering yourselves in twenty years' time, on a piece of yellowed cardboard (yellowed emotionally, even if modern printing procedures will preserve it unchanged). The taste for the spontaneous, natural, lifelike snapshot kills spontaneity, drives away the present. Photographed reality immediately takes on a nostalgic character, of joy fled on the wings of time, a commemorative quality, even if the picture was taken the day before yesterday.

And the life that you live in order to photograph it is already, at the outset, a commemoration of itself. To believe that the snapshot is more *true* than the posed portrait is a prejudice. . . ."

So saying, Antonino darted around the two girls in the water, to focus on the movements of their game and cut out of the picture the dazzling glints of the sun on the water. In a scuffle for the ball, Bice, flinging herself on the other girl, who was submerged, was snapped with her behind in close-up, flying over the waves. Antonino, so as not to lose this angle, had flung himself back in the water while holding up the camera, nearly drowning.

"They all came out well, and this one's stupendous," they commented a few days later, snatching the proofs from each other. They had arranged to meet at the photography shop. "You're good; you must take some more of us."

Antonino had reached the conclusion that it was necessary to return to posed subjects, in attitudes denoting their social position and their character, as in the nineteenth century. His antiphotographic polemic could be fought only from within the black box, setting one kind of photography against another.

"I'd like to have one of those old box cameras," he said to his girl-friends, "the kind you put on a tripod. Do you think it's still possible to find one?"

"Hmm, maybe at some junk shop . . ."

"Let's go see."

The girls found it amusing to hunt for this curious object; to-gether they ransacked flea markets, interrogated old street photogra-phers, followed them to their lairs. In those cemeteries of objects no longer serviceable lay wooden columns, screens, backdrops with faded landscapes; everything that suggested an old photographer's studio, Antonino bought. In the end he managed to get hold of a box cam-era, with a bulb to squeeze. It seemed in perfect working order. An-tonino also bought an assortment of plates. With the girls helping him, he set up the studio in a room of his apartment, all fitted out with old-fashioned equipment, except for two modern spotlights.

Now he was content. "This is where to start," he explained to the girls. "In the way our grandparents assumed a pose, in the convention that decided how groups were to be arranged, there was a social meaning, a custom, a taste, a culture. An official photograph, or one of a marriage or a family or a school group, conveyed how serious and important each role or institution was, but also how far they were all false or forced, authoritarian, hierarchical. This is the point: to make explicit the relationship with the world that each of us bears within himself, and which today we tend to hide, to make unconscious, believing that in this way it disappears, whereas . . ."

"Who do you want to have pose for you?"

"You two come tomorrow, and I'll begin by taking some pictures of you in the way I mean."

"Say, what's in the back of your mind?" Lydia asked, suddenly suspicious. Only now, as the studio was all set up, did she see that everything about it had a sinister, threatening air. "If you think we're going to come and be your models, you're dreaming!"

Bice giggled with her, but the next day she came back to Antonino's apartment, alone.

She was wearing a white linen dress with colored embroidery on the edges of the sleeves and pockets. Her hair was parted and gathered over her temples. She laughed, a bit slyly, bending her head to one side. As he let her in, Antonino studied her manner — a bit coy, a bit ironic — to discover what were the traits that defined her true character.

He made her sit in a big armchair, and stuck his head under the black cloth that came with his camera. It was one of those boxes whose rear wall was of glass, where the image is reflected as if already on the plate, ghostly, a bit milky, deprived of every link with space and time. To Antonino it was as if he had never seen Bice before. She had a docility in her somewhat heavy way of lowering her eyelids, of stretching her neck forward, that promised something hidden, as her smile seemed to hide behind the very act of smiling.

"There. Like that. No, head a bit farther; raise your eyes. No, lower them." Antonino was pursuing, within that box, something of Bice that all at once seemed most precious to him, absolute.

"Now you're casting a shadow; move into the light. No, it was better before."

There were many possible photographs of Bice and many Bices impossible to photograph, but what he was seeking was the unique photograph that would contain both the former and the latter.

"I can't get you," his voice emerged, stifled and complaining from beneath the black hood, "I can't get you any more; I can't manage to get you."

He freed himself from the cloth and straightened up again. He was going about it all wrong. That expression, that accent, that secret he seemed on the very point of capturing in her face, was something that drew him into the quicksands of moods, humors, psychology: he, too, was one of those who pursue life as it flees, a hunter of the unattainable, like the takers of snapshots.

He had to follow the opposite path: aim at a portrait completely on the surface, evident, unequivocal, that did not elude conventional appearance, the stereotype, the mask. The mask, being first of all a social, historical product, contains more truth than any image claiming to be "true"; it bears a quantity of meanings that will gradually be revealed. Wasn't this precisely Antonino's intention in setting up this fair booth of a studio?

He observed Bice. He should start with the exterior elements of her appearance. In Bice's way of dressing and fixing herself up – he thought – you could recognize the somewhat nostalgic, somewhat ironic intention, widespread in the mode of those years, to hark back

to the fashions of thirty years earlier. The photograph should under-
line this intention: why hadn't he thought of that?

Antonino went to find a tennis racket; Bice should stand up in a
three-quarter turn, the racket under her arm, her face in the pose of a
sentimental postcard. To Antonino, from under the black drape,
Bice's image – in its slimness and suitability to the pose, and in the
unsuitable and almost incongruous aspects that the pose accentuated
– seemed very interesting. He made her change position several
times, studying the geometry of legs and arms in relation to the racket and to some element in the background. (In the ideal postcard in
his mind there would have been the net of the tennis court, but you
couldn't demand too much, and Antonino made do with a Ping-
Pong table.)

But he still didn't feel on safe ground: wasn't he perhaps trying to
photograph memories – or, rather, vague echoes of recollection
surfacing in the memory? Wasn't his refusal to live the present as a
future memory, as the Sunday photographers did, leading him to
attempt an equally unreal operation, namely to give a body to recollection, to substitute it for the present before his very eyes?

"Move! Don't stand there like a stick! Raise the racket, damn it!
Pretend you're playing tennis!" All of a sudden he was furious. He
had realized that only by exaggerating the poses could he achieve an
objective alienness; only by feigning a movement arrested halfway
could he give the impression of the unmoving, the nonliving.

Bice obediently followed his orders even when they became vague
and contradictory, with a passivity that was also a way of declaring
herself out of the game, and yet somehow insinuating, in this game
that was not hers, the unpredictable moves of a mysterious match of
her own. What Antonino now was expecting of Bice, telling her to
put her legs and arms this way and that way, was not so much the
simple performance of a plan as her response to the violence he was

doing her with his demands, an unforeseeable aggressive reply to this violence that he was being driven more and more to wreak on her.

It was like a dream, Antonino thought, contemplating, from the darkness in which he was buried, that improbable tennis player filtered into the glass rectangle: like a dream when a presence coming from the depth of memory advances, is recognized, and then suddenly is transformed into something unexpected, something that even before the transformation is already frightening because there's no telling what it might be transformed into.

Did he want to photograph dreams? This suspicion struck him dumb, hidden in that ostrich refuge of his with the bulb in his hand, like an idiot; and meanwhile Bice, left to herself, continued a kind of grotesque dance, freezing in exaggerated tennis poses, backhand, drive, raising the racket high or lowering it to the ground as if the gaze coming from that glass eye were the ball she continued to slam back.

"Stop, what's this nonsense? This isn't what I had in mind." Antonino covered the camera with the cloth and began pacing up and down the room.

It was all the fault of that dress, with its tennis, prewar connotations. . . . It had to be admitted that if she wore a street dress the kind of photograph he described couldn't be taken. A certain solemnity was needed, a certain pomp, like the official photos of queens. Only in evening dress would Bice become a photographic subject, with the décolleté that marks a distinct line between the white of the skin and the darkness of the fabric, accentuated by the glitter of jewels, a boundary between an essence of woman, almost atemporal and almost impersonal in her nakedness, and the other abstraction, social this time, the dress, symbol of an equally impersonal role, like the drapery of an allegorical statue.

He approached Bice, began to unbutton the dress at the neck and over the bosom, and slip it down over her shoulders. He had thought of certain nineteenth-century photographs of women in which from the white of the cardboard emerge the face, the neck, the line of the bared shoulders, while all the rest disappears into the whiteness.

This was the portrait outside of time and space that he now wanted; he wasn't quite sure how it was achieved, but he was determined to succeed. He set the spotlight on Bice, moved the camera closer, fiddled around under the cloth adjusting the aperture of the lens. He looked into it. Bice was naked.

She had made the dress slip down to her feet; she wasn't wearing anything underneath it; she had taken a step forward – no, a step backward, which was as if her whole body were advancing in the picture; she stood erect, tall before the camera, calm, looking straight ahead, as if she were alone.

Antonino felt the sight of her enter his eyes and occupy the whole visual field, removing it from the flux of casual and fragmentary images, concentrating time and space in a finite form. And as if this visual surprise and the impression of the plate were two reflexes connected among themselves, he immediately pressed the bulb, loaded the camera again, snapped, put in another plate, snapped, and went on changing plates and snapping, mumbling, stifled by the cloth, "There, that's right now, yes, again, I'm getting you fine now, another."

He had run out of plates. He emerged from the cloth. He was pleased. Bice was before him, naked, as if waiting.

"Now you can dress," he said, euphoric, but already in a hurry. "Let's go out."

She looked at him, bewildered.

"I've got you now," he said.

Bice burst into tears.

Antonino realized that he had fallen in love with her that same day. They started living together, and he bought the most modern cameras, telescopic lens, the most advanced equipment; he installed a darkroom. He even had a set-up for photographing her when she was asleep at night. Bice would wake at the flash, annoyed; Antonino went on taking snapshots of her disentangling herself from sleep, of her becoming furious with him, of her trying in vain to find sleep again by plunging her face into the pillow, of her making up with him, of her recognizing as acts of love these photographic rapes.

In Antonino's darkroom, strung with films and proofs, Bice peered from every frame, as thousands of bees peer out from the honeycomb of a hive, but always the same bee: Bice in every attitude, at every angle, in every guise, Bice posed or caught unaware, an identity fragmented into a powder of images.

"But what's this obsession with Bice? Can't you photograph anything else?" was the question he heard constantly from his friends, and also from her.

"It isn't just a matter of Bice," he answered. "It's a question of method. Whatever person you decide to photograph, or whatever thing, you must go on photographing it always, exclusively, at every hour of the day and night. Photography has a meaning only if it exhausts all possible images."

But he didn't say what meant most to him: to catch Bice in the street when she didn't know he was watching her, to keep her in the range of hidden lenses, to photograph her not only without letting himself be seen but without seeing her, to surprise her as she was in the absence of his gaze, of any gaze. Not that he wanted to discover any particular thing; he wasn't a jealous man in the usual sense of the word. It was an invisible Bice that he wanted to possess, a Bice absolutely alone, a Bice whose presence presupposed the absence of him and everyone else.

Whether or not it could be defined as jealousy, it was, in any case, a passion difficult to put up with. And soon Bice left him.

Antonino sank into deep depression. He began to keep a diary – a photographic diary, of course. With the camera slung around his neck, shut up in the house, slumped in an armchair, he compulsively snapped pictures as he stared into the void. He was photographing the absence of Bice.

He collected the photographs in an album: you could see ashtrays brimming with cigarette butts, an unmade bed, a damp stain on the wall. He got the idea of composing a catalogue of everything in the world that resists photography, that is systematically omitted from the visual field not only by cameras but also by human beings. On every subject he spent days, using up whole rolls at intervals of hours, so as to follow the changes of light and shadow. One day he became obsessed with a completely empty corner of the room, containing a radiator pipe and nothing else: he was tempted to go on photograph-ing that spot and only that till the end of his days.

The apartment was completely neglected; old newspapers, letters lay crumpled on the floor, and he photographed them. The pho-tographs in the papers were photographed as well, and an indirect bond was established between his lens and that of distant news pho-tographers. To produce those black spots the lenses of other cameras had been aimed at police assaults, charred automobiles, running ath-letes, ministers, defendants.

Antonino now felt a special pleasure in portraying domestic objects framed by a mosaic of telephotos, violent patches of ink on white sheets. From his immobility he was surprised to find he envied the life of the news photographer, who moves following the move-ments of crowds, bloodshed, tears, feasts, crime, the conventions of fashion, the falsity of official ceremonies; the news photographer, who documents the extremes of society, the richest and the poorest, the exceptional moments that are nevertheless produced at every moment and in every place.

Does this mean that only the exceptional condition has a meaning? Antonino asked himself. Is the news photographer the true antagonist of the Sunday photographer? Are their worlds mutually exclusive? Or does the one give meaning to the other?

Reflecting like this, he began to tear up the photographs with Bice or without Bice that had accumulated during the months of his passion, ripping to pieces the strips of proofs hung on the walls, snipping up the celluloid of the negatives, jabbing the slides, and piling the remains of this methodical destruction on newspapers spread out on the floor.

Perhaps true, total photography, he thought, is a pile of fragments of private images, against the creased background of massacres and coronations.

He folded the corners of the newspapers into a huge bundle to be thrown into the trash, but first he wanted to photograph it. He arranged the edges so that you could clearly see two halves of photographs from different newspapers that in the bundle happened, by chance, to fit together. In fact he reopened the package a little so that a bit of shiny pasteboard would stick out, the fragment of a torn enlargement. He turned on a spotlight; he wanted it to be possible to recognize in his photograph the half-crumpled and torn images, and at the same time to feel their unreality as casual, inky shadows, and also at the same time their concreteness as objects charged with meaning, the strength with which they clung to the attention that tried to drive them away.

To get all this into one photograph he had to acquire an extraordinary technical skill, but only then would Antonino quit taking pictures. Having exhausted every possibility, at the moment when he was coming full circle Antonino realized that photographing photographs was the only course that he had left – or, rather, the true course he had obscurely been seeking all this time.

Notes on the Authors and Photographers

Authors

HOB BROUN (1950–1987) published his first novel, *Odditorium*, in 1983. While writing his second, *Inner Tube*, he underwent surgery on a spinal tumor which left him paralyzed from the neck down and unable to breathe without a respirator. He completed the book by blowing air through a tube connected to his computer keyboard. Broun's last works were collected as *Cardinal Numbers*, published posthumously in 1988.

ITALO CALVINO (1923–1987) was an Italian novelist, essayist, and fabulist whose style ranged from the realism of his debut novel, *The Path to the Nest of Spiders*, to the experimentalism of *If on a winter's night a traveler*. "The Adventure of a Photographer" appeared in his 1983 collection *Difficult Loves*. Calvino's other books include *Cosmicomics*, *Invisible Cities*, and *Italian Folktales*, an anthology of traditional fables.

JULIO CORTÁZAR (1914–1984) was born in Brussels to Argentinean parents and grew up in Buenos Aires. In 1952 he moved to Paris, where he lived for the rest of his life. His 1963 novel *Hopscotch* is often credited with sparking worldwide interest in Latin American literature. Among his other books are *A Change of Light*, *The End of the Game*, *We Love Glenda So Much*, and *A Certain Lucas*. "Blow-Up" was adapted into a celebrated film by Michelangelo Antonioni.

RICK DEMARINIS (b. 1934) is the author of six novels, including *The Mortician's Apprentice* and *The Year of the Zinc Penny*, and four collections of short stories. "Billy Ducks Among the Pharoahs" appeared in his 1986 collection *Under the Wheat*.

DORRIS DÖRRIE (b. 1955) is a German film director and short story writer best known for her 1986 film *Men. . .* , an international success and the biggest home-grown box-office hit in West Germany since World War II. Dörrie is also the author of the story collections *Love, Pain, and the Whole Damn Thing* and *What Do You Want from Me?*

ALBERTO MORAVIA (1907–1990) was an Italian novelist, journalist, and short story writer whose first novel, *The Time of Indifference*, was published to wide acclaim in Europe when he was only twenty-two. His later works include *The Woman of Rome, Disobedience, The Conformist*, and *Time of Desecration*.

CYNTHIA OZICK (b. 1928) is the author of the novels *Trust, The Cannibal Galaxy, The Messiah of Stockholm*, and *The Shawl*, as well as several volumes of short stories, including *Levitation: Five Fictions*, in which "Shots" appeared. Her third book of essays, *Fame and Folly*, was published in 1996.

V. S. PRITCHETT (b. 1900) was knighted in 1975 for his many contributions to English letters – in the form of short stories, novels, biography, criticism, travel books, and memoirs. His stories have been collected in more than a dozen volumes, including *When My Girl Comes Home, The Key to My Heart, Blind Love*, and *The Camberwell Beauty*. Among his novels are *Clare Drummer, Dead Man Leading*, and *Mr. Beluncle*. His nonfiction works include biographies of Balzac, Turgenev, and Chekhov, and two memoirs, *A Cab at the Door* and *Midnight Oil*.

E. ANNIE PROULX (b. 1935) is the author of the novels *The Shipping News*, for which she received the National Book Award and the Pulitzer Prize, *Postcards*, and the collection *Heart Songs and Other Stories*. Her latest novel is *Accordion Crimes*.

PAUL THEROUX (b. 1941) was a foreign service officer before becoming a novelist and travel writer. His novels include *Waldo, Saint Jack, Picture Palace, The Mosquito Coast*, and *My Secret History*. He has also written short stories, plays, and critical essays. Theroux's footloose travels by rail and sea have been recounted in *The Great Railway Bazaar, The Old Patagonian Express, Sailing Through China*, and *The Happy Isles of Oceania*, among others. His most recent book is *My Other Life*.

Photographers

ROSSELLA BELLUSCI (b. 1947) was born in San Lorenzo del Vallo, Italy. Trained as a psychologist, she began her photographic career with a Milan press agency. Her subsequent work comprises self-portraiture, fashion, and still lifes. Her photographs are in the collections of the Musée National d'Art Moderne in Paris and the Museum of Modern Art in New York, among others.

BILL BRANDT (1904–1983) was born in London and began his career in Paris in 1929 as an apprentice to Man Ray. In the 1930s, he published two books of social observation, *The English at Home* and *A Night in London*. His later work included portraits of leading artists and writers, landscapes, and an extended series of stark, often distorted nudes, published in *Perspective of Nudes* and *Shadow of Light*.

ROBERT CUMMING (b. 1943) is a painter, sculptor, and conceptual photographer. His wry, mock-scientific photographs, often presented as diptychs, ruminate on the chasm between photographic representation and reality. *Robert Cumming: Photographic Works 1969–1980* was issued in 1994.

JACK DELANO (b. 1914) is a photographer, filmmaker, composer, teacher, and designer. Born in Russia and educated in Philadelphia, he is best known as a photographer for his work for the Farm Security Administration between 1941 and 1943. Since 1946, he has lived in Puerto Rico.

HAROLD E. EDGERTON (b. 1903) is the inventor of the electronic flash. His most famous photographs capture movements too fleeting for the human eye – such as a milk drop caught mid-splash – or render athletic feats in single-frame, multiple-flash exposures. Trained as an electircal engineer, Edgerton pioneered nighttime aerial reconnaissance during World War II, photographed H-bomb tests in 1952, and made signal contributions to underwater photography, working for many years with Jacques Cousteau. His photographs have been published in *Stopping Time: The Photographs of Harold Edgerton*, among other books.

WALKER EVANS (1903–1975) mixed architectural views, portraiture, and social reportage in a landmark 1938 book, *American Photographs*, arguably the first book of photography to isolate a uniquely American iconography. Other books of his work published during his lifetime include his collaboration with the writer James Agee, *Let Us Now Praise Famous Men*, and *Message from the Interior*.

VANCE GELLERT (b. 1944) is compiling an extended series of photographs about fatherhood, some of which appeared in his 1987 book *CarlVision*. A cofounder of pARTs Photographic Arts in Minneapolis, he teaches at Minneapolis College of Art and Design.

ALLEN GINSBERG (b. 1926), a leading poet of the Beat movement, has been taking photographs since the 1940s. His affectionate glimpses of his counterculture peers – the writers Jack Kerouac, William Burroughs, and Gregory Corso; the photographer Robert Frank; and others – have been collected in the books *Allen Ginsberg: Photographs* and *Snapshot Poetics.*

DAVID GRAHAM (b. 1952) has published the books *American Beauty* and *Only in America*, which celebrate American roadside culture. His editorial work has appeared in *The New York Times Magazine, Details, Esquire, Time,* and other publications.

O. WINSTON LINK (b. 1914) was educated as a civil engineer before becoming a commercial photographer. Between 1955 and 1960 he created a rhapsodic record of steam railroading in North Carolina and the Virginias, often working at night with intricate lighting. His dramatic views of hurtling locomotives and small-town life along the tracks have been collected in *Steam, Steel & Stars* and *The Last Steam Railroad in America.*

Weegee (1928–1987), born Arthur Fellig, was a colorful New York news photographer whose nickname referred to his Ouija-like gravitation to crime scenes, fires, and other urban calamities. Born in Austria, he worked as a tintype operator and a photographer's assistant before free-lancing for the *Daily News*, the *Post*, the *Herald Tribune*, and other news-papers and magazines. His books include *Naked City* and *Weegee by Weegee: An Autobiography*.

Jack Welpott (b. 1923) is known for landscapes, portraits, and nudes that combine formal equipoise and mystery. He was born in Kansas City, Missouri, attended college and graduate school in Indiana, and in 1959 moved to San Francisco, where he taught photography at San Francisco State University for thirty-three years. A retrospective of his work, *Jack Welpott: The Halide Conversion*, was published in 1988.

Garry Winogrand (1928–1984) used quick, teeming, and sometimes tilted 35mm compositions to reveal off-kilter aspects of American public life. His books include *The Animals*, *Women Are Beautiful*, *Public Relations*, and *Stock Photographs: The Fort Worth Fat Stock Show and Rodeo*.

———

The publisher gratefully acknowledges permission to reprint the following material from the following sources.

"The Image Trade" from *The Complete Collected Stories of V. S. Pritchett* by V. S. Pritchett. Copyright © 1991 by V. S. Pritchett. Reprinted by permission of Random House, Inc.

"Billy Ducks Among the Pharaohs" from *Under the Wheat*, by Rick DeMarinis. Copyright © 1986 by Rick DeMarinis. Reprinted by permission of the University of Pittsburgh Press.

"Highspeed Linear Main St." from *Cardinal Numbers* by Hob Broun. Copyright © 1988 by the Estate of Hob Broun. Reprinted by permission of Alfred A. Knopf, Inc.

"Negatives" from *Heart Songs and Other Stories* by E. Annie Proulx. Copyright © 1988, 1995 by E. Annie Proulx. Reprinted with the permission of Scribner, an imprint of Simon & Schuster.

"Shots" from *Levitation* by Cynthia Ozick. Copyright © 1982 by Cynthia Ozick. Reprinted by permission of Alfred A. Knopf, Inc.

"The Swollen Face" from *The Fetish and Other Stories* by Alberto Moravia. Copyright © 1962 by RCS Libri & Grandi Opera SpA, Milano. I edizione Bompiani 1962.

"Greene" from *Picture Palace* (Houghton Mifflin) by Paul Theroux. Copyright © 1978 by Paul Theroux. Reprinted with the permission of Wylie, Aitken & Stone, Inc.

"Lies" from *What Do You Want From Me?* by Dorris Dörrie. Copyright © 1991 by Alfred A. Knopf, Inc. Reprinted by permission of the publisher.

"Blow-Up" from *End of the Game and Other Stories* by Julio Cortázar, translated by Paul Blackburn. Copyright © 1967, 1963 by Random House, Inc. Reprinted by per-mission of Pantheon Books, a division of Random House, Inc.

"The Adventure of a Photographer" from *Difficult Loves* by Italo Calvino. Copyright 1949 by Giulio Einaudi editore, Torino. English translation copyright © 1984 by Harcourt Brace & Company. Reproduced by permission of Harcourt Brace & Company.